T. W. WEST

Discovering English Architecture

with revisions by
Tim Buxbaum

SHIRE PUBLICATIONS LTD

Published in 2000 by Shire Publications Ltd, Cromwell House, Church Street, Princes Risborough, Buckinghamshire HP27 9AJ, UK. Website: www.shirebooks.co.uk

Copyright © 1979 by T. W. West and 1993 by Tim Buxbaum. First published 1979; reprinted 1984 and 1988. Reprinted with new material by Tim Buxbaum in 1993 and 2000. Number 244 in the Discovering series. ISBN 0 85263 455 2.

This text, here revised and updated in 1979 with new photographs and bibliography, formed the basis of 'Architecture in England' published by The English Universities Press Ltd (Teach Yourself Books). The last chapter, glossary, gazetteer and bibliography of the present edition were revised by Tim Buxbaum in 1993 and 2000.

Printed in Great Britain by CIT Printing Services Ltd, Press Buildings, Merlins Bridge, Haverfordwest, Pembrokeshire SA61 1XF.

ACKNOWLEDGEMENTS

Photographs are acknowledged as follows: John Anthony, plate 35; Robert D. Bristow, plates 24, 28; British Tourist Authority, plate 22; Tim Buxbaum, plates 50, 54, 56, 61, 62, 67, 69, 72; Martin Charles, plate 63; Terry Farrell & Co Ltd (photographer Nigel Young), plate 73; Foster Associates, plate 66; George H. Haines, plates 14 (by kind permission of the Vicar and Churchwardens of St Mary's, Warwick), 25; Hunt Thompson Associates, plate 70; Cadbury Lamb, plates 1, 2, 4, 5, 7, 9, 13, 15, 16, 18, 20, 21, 23, 26, 27, 30, 32, 36-8, 40-3, 46, 48, 49, 51-3, 55, 57, 59, 60, 68, 71; Levitt Bernstein Associates, plate 64; MacCormac Jamieson & Pritchard, plate 65; Mimram Studio, plate 45; National Monuments Record, plate 34; Eileen Preston, plate 58; Sotheby Parke Bernet & Co, plate 47; David Uttley, plates 6, 11, 12, 17; Jeffery Whitelaw, plates 3, 10, 19, 29, 31, 44; Geoffrey N. Wright, plates 8, 33, 39.

The cover photograph by Cadbury Lamb is of Marble Hill House, Twickenham.

MODEL DWELLING FOR ARTISANS,
GREAT EXHIBITION 1851

Contents

THE HISTORICAL STYLES OF ENGLISH ARCHITECTURE

— 43	Prehistoric	
43-450	Roman	
450-1066		Romanesque 450-1190
1066-1190	Anglo-Norman	
1190-1290	Early English	
1290-1375	Decorated	Gothic 1190-1485
1375-1485	Perpendicular	
1485-1558	Tudor	
1558-1603	Elizabethan	
1603-1625	Jacobean	Renaissance 1558-1702
1625-1702	Stuart	
1695-1725	Baroque	
1720-1760	Palladian	
1760-1800	Adam	Georgian 1702-1837
1810-1837	Regency	
1837-1901	Victorian	
1901-1910	Edwardian	

These dates give a convenient classification though to some extent the styles overlap the periods. The term 'Palladian' is also applied to the work of Inigo Jones in the seventeenth century. 'Queen Anne' strictly describes the domestic architecture of Queen Anne's reign, 1702-14; but it can be used more loosely to include work of the last fifteen years of the seventeenth century, or alternatively to signify 'early Georgian'.

MOUND OF EARTH   FLAGGED OR CORBELLED ROOF

CHAMBERED BARROW

CORBELLING TO
FORM A ROOF

GREEK

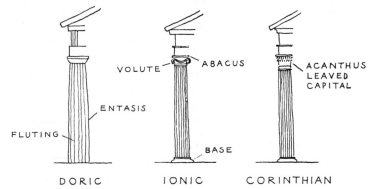

VOLUTE — ABACUS

ACANTHUS
LEAVED
CAPITAL

ENTASIS

FLUTING

BASE

DORIC   IONIC   CORINTHIAN

ROMAN

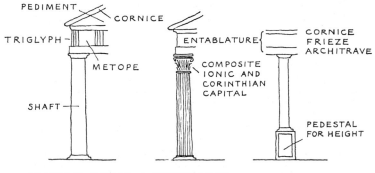

PEDIMENT
CORNICE
TRIGLYPH
METOPE
ENTABLATURE

CORNICE
FRIEZE
ARCHITRAVE

COMPOSITE
IONIC AND
CORINTHIAN
CAPITAL

SHAFT

PEDESTAL
FOR HEIGHT

TUSCAN DORIC   COMPOSITE

4

1. Prehistoric and Roman

Architecture in prehistoric Britain

Before the Roman Conquest little that was built could be called architecture. There must have been various simple types of wattle shelters in use but the oldest stone structures are the remains of megalithic monuments, the greatest being Stonehenge. Stone circles such as these reveal a primitive sense of ceremonial planning, but they are scarcely buildings.

The first claim might be made for the neolithic chambered tomb with its flagged or corbelled roof heaped over with earth or, better still, for the dry stone wall dwellings of early bronze-age date at Skara Brae in the Orkneys, with their built-in furniture of flagstones and, again, a corbelled roof. But the commonest prehistoric structures seem to have been the circular huts whose bronze-age foundations are to be found in various parts of England, and which with their turf or thatch roofs continued to serve as the standard dwelling of the Briton throughout the Roman period.

Sometimes hut circles are found in villages within the concentric ditches of iron-age hillforts, though the earliest earthworks were the neolithic causeway-camps. The great ditches of the hillforts followed the contours of the ground and above them in their heyday rose earth and stone ramparts surmounted by timber stockades. Access to the central enclosure was across the ditches by causeways carefully staggered to hinder the approach of an attacker. The finest of these fortified settlements was Maiden Castle in Dorset, which finally fell to the Roman invader.

An example of a stone-built iron-age village which continued in occupation into the Roman period may be seen at Chysauster near Penzance. There are the remains of four pairs of houses built of granite rubble masonry and arranged across a cobbled street. Each house consisted of an open courtyard surrounded by a circular wall, in the thickness of which were rooms opening inwards. Floors were paved and roofs corbelled or thatched.

Roman architecture

The Romans brought with them a fully developed building technique, the expression of that practical engineering skill for which they are famed. Their system of construction sprang from two sources: the Greek column and beam system; and the arch, vault and dome of the Etruscans.

They took over from the Greeks the three orders of pillar and beam construction and added two of their own. In each order the proportions and details of columns, capitals and entablatures were all different. The most frequent are the Tuscan Doric, with its slimmer, unfluted shaft, and the Corinthian, its capital richly decorated with an acanthus-leaf motif. But in a manner quite unknown to the Greeks the Romans frequently applied their orders to what was basically a pier and arch structure, thus using them in a purely decorative manner as well as in the orthodox way.

An important technical innovation was their use of concrete, a mixture of stone fragments and lime which could be made anywhere without the need for skilled labour. It was particularly useful for the construction of cross and barrel vaults, domes and even walls which were then faced with stone or brick.

Openings were generally semicircular or square-headed; roofs were low-pitched and covered with tiles, which the Romans introduced to England together with the knowledge of brickmaking. Embellishment of all kinds was a feature of Roman buildings, and decorative effects were obtained in numerous ways. Facings on walls enhanced as well as protected them if made of attractive stone, marble, brickwork or mosaic. Interior surfaces were stuccoed and adorned with mural paintings framed by painted

SUPERIMPOSED ORDERS APPLIED
DECORATIVELY TO A PIER AND ARCH SYSTEM

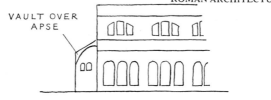

VAULT OVER APSE

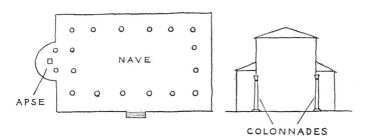

APSE

NAVE

COLONNADES

ROMAN BASILICA

pilasters. Floors were of stone, marble, tiles, herringbone brick-work or tessellated with mosaic. Statues were placed in wall niches or on roof-lines or at pediment angles, while there was much rather coarse and florid carving, the commonest motifs being acanthus, ox-heads, and garlands of fruit and flowers.

The general feeling was one of mass rather than space: Roman architecture was heavy and plastic. At its best it had a gravity and dignified grandeur expressive of Roman power; at its worst it was ostentatious and vulgar. But Britain was one of the provinces furthest from Rome and its buildings were very much smaller, simpler and less grand than those we know existed in Italy.

Former tribal centres like Verulamium (St Albans), which began as a Belgic settlement, became typical Roman towns. Most were well sited. Some survived, such as Chester and York; others like Verulamium and Silchester (Hampshire) were later abandoned.

The most characteristic buildings were secular, connected with the administration and with social life. Public buildings were sometimes constructed with imported marble. They stressed the political importance of the town as well as its economic function.

Street plans were usually rectilinear, with the building blocks grouped in the spaces between and separated by footways. An outer wall was provided with battlements and gateways, and it was surrounded by a *fosse* or ditch. At the main intersection was the forum, serving as market place and civic centre and the focus of town life. Rectangular and surrounded by basilicas, temples, baths, shops and peristyles (colonnades), it affords the earliest example of town planning: the design of a group of buildings in their spatial relationship to one another.

Basilicas were public assembly halls and served as town halls, law courts and commercial exchanges. Rectangular in plan, they consisted of a nave with two (sometimes four) aisles separated by Corinthian colonnades carried right across the nave at both ends making a complete ambulatory. In one of the short walls was a semicircular apse, containing a dais with wallseats or altar, also screened off by a colonnade from the main body of the hall. The roof was of timber which covered a coffered timber ceiling, and the plain exterior usually contrasted with the rich decoration within. At Silchester the basilica was 230 feet by 60 feet (70.1m by 18.3m) with an apse at both ends, and it occupied the west side of a forum 300 feet (91.4m) square.

Temples dedicated to the pagan gods of Rome were either rectangular or square. The *cella* or chamber was usually raised on a platform or *podium* and surrounded by a range of half columns (Corinthian at the temple of Sulis Minerva, Bath) 'supporting' a cornice and pedimented roof. A flight of steps led up to a deep

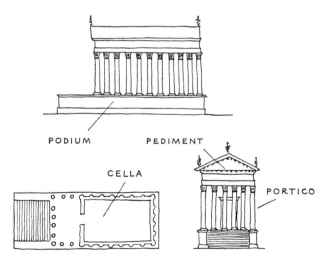

PODIUM   PEDIMENT

CELLA

PORTICO

portico of freestanding columns and sometimes there was an apse at the rear. Floors were tessellated with an altar or cult object in the centre or on a dais in the apse. Ceilings were vaulted or of coffered timber. The first stone building of any size

SCHEMATISED PLAN OF THERMAE

		3	1	
6	5	4	2	
			7	

1 UNDRESSING ROOM

2 TEPIARUM, WARM
  CHAMBER OR LOUNGE

3 & 4 SUDATORIA, HOT
  AIR ROOMS

5 & 6 CALDARIA, HOT
  WATER BATHS

7 FRIGIDARIUM, COLD
  WATER SWIMMING POOL

ALSO OILING & MASSAGE
ROOMS, HYPOCAUSTS,
FURNACES ETC.

in Britain was the temple of Claudius at Colchester (AD 50), its mound now occupied by the remains of a Norman castle rising from massive Roman concrete vaults.

Hot baths or *thermae* played a central part in Roman life, for in addition to their contribution to health and hygiene they acted as social centres. Similar in principle, they varied greatly in size and details of planning. The schematised plan shows one arrangement of the main elements.

The baths at Aquae Sulis (Bath) had an open-air swimming pool 80 feet by 40 feet (24.4m by 12.2m) and 6 feet (1.8m) deep, lined with lead from the Mendip Hills and surrounded by a roofed pavement with stone steps down to the water. Later the pool was covered by a barrel vault of hollow box-tiles supported on 40 foot (12.2m) columns. It was provided with a culvert drain.

Certain chambers were heated by means of a *hypocaust* or cellar into which glowing charcoal was pushed from a stoking chamber. The hot air and gases warmed the cement floor above (raised on pillars of tiles) and passed through terracotta flue pipes up the walls to be discharged under the eaves.

Theatres to accommodate public sports were built close outside the towns. By the second century Verulamium had one for plays and circus performances of animal fights and gladiatorial combats. The auditorium was open to the sky with tiers of stone seats enclosing a circular area 80 feet (24.4m) in diameter. It was often hollowed out of a slope, raised on concrete vaulting or, as here, excavated, the upcast forming a bank for the seats. Entrance was by means of vaulted tunnels. The theatre derived from the Greeks but the amphitheatre (two semicircular theatres brought together) was a Roman invention. It was essentially for combat.

Roman domestic buildings may be considered under two heads:

town and country. Town houses varied in size. The medium-sized *domus* had plain façades with perhaps shops on the street frontage. Amenities were good for the time. Windows were of glass but most light came from above a central court. The front door had a mortice lock, the roof was tiled and the principal rooms were heated with braziers. Larger houses had central heating by *hypocaust* and the luxury of tessellated floors. Sometimes house plans were L-shaped or of the corridor type with rooms opening off a passage. Slaves occupied *insulae*, storeyed like tenements or barracks.

Romano-British country houses or villas were centres of large farming estates growing corn for the towns and the army. They were constructed of half timber raised on stone footings and when complete must have resembled Tudor buildings of similar design. Another point of resemblance was the way the courtyard type had its ranges of rooms along three or four sides of a quadrangular court, though opening on to pent-roofed verandas.

The main block consisted of living-rooms, bedrooms and offices, with a central hall placed opposite the entrance. The side blocks contained the quarters of the servants and slaves and the barns, granaries, threshing floors and workshops necessary for a large farm. Some villas were equipped with a heated corn-drying floor, an innovation useful in a damp climate, and a large walled farmyard was frequently attached. As with the larger town houses the best rooms had tessellated floors, patterned or pictorial, and were decorated with frescoes and heated by *hypocaust*.

A second type of villa was the corridor type. The plan was simpler with a single range of rooms opening off a colonnaded veranda; sometimes a pair of side blocks or short wings was added. A few larger courtyard villas had corridors both inside and outside the quadrangle, thus combining the two kinds of plan, as at Folkestone. Upper storeys are conjectural.

Small villas resembling manor houses or farmsteads were of the columned barn type, with a nave and two aisles divided off by timber posts supporting the roof. Rooms were constructed inside or built on at the end and floors were of rammed earth. Being less substantial, however, fewer of these have survived.

At Silchester are remains, unique in England, of a small fifth-century early Christian basilica, probably derived from the hall or basilica of a private villa and first used as a chapel when in 312 under Constantine Christianity became the state religion. Such buildings as this were the prototypes of the basilican church of the middle ages.

Towns had stone walls in the late third century, but the greatest monument to Roman military power, Hadrian's Wall, goes back to the early second century. Constructed of concrete faced with stone, it ran from Tyne to Solway, punctuated at intervals by mile-

EARLY CHRISTIAN
CHURCH
SILCHESTER

castles (guard-posts) and smaller turrets or watchtowers. In the
hills to the south it was supported by a network of roads and forts.

These forts or *castella* of 2½ to 5 acres (1 to 2 ha) occurred
at intervals of about five miles (8km). Similar ones were built
elsewhere in the interior at strategic points of the internal communication system. Basically they were square or rectangular
enclosures with rounded corners and battlemented ramparts of
stone or turf faced with stone. Each wall was provided with a
gateway, angle and interval towers, and round the outside ran a
berm and ditch of V-section. At the principal intersection stood
the *principia* or headquarters building and a shrine. Nearby were
the *praetorium* (commandant's villa), officers' quarters, stores and
granaries with supplies for a year or two. Further away were the
long barrack and stable buildings. At Housesteads (Borcovicium)
there was a bath-house that served as a recreation centre outside
the walls.

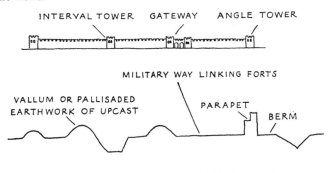

SECTION THROUGH HADRIAN'S WALL

After Rome was sacked in 410 Britain was gradually left to itself
to suffer the Teutonic incursions. The Saxons usually preferred
their own sites to those of the Romans, whose towns and buildings
slowly perished through disuse.

2. Romanesque

Romanesque is the stylistic name given to the architecture of western Europe in the period between the break-up of the Roman Empire and the coming of Gothic towards the end of the twelfth century. Its two principal sources were the surviving architecture of Rome, particularly the Christian basilicas, and the Byzantine style of the Eastern Empire. Anglo-Saxon and Anglo-Norman architecture were local variations of Romanesque.

Anglo-Saxon architecture

The earliest Saxon buildings were built of timber, like the great hall described in the *Beowulf* saga. At Yeavering (Northumberland) an Anglo-Saxon township of the seventh century had both a stone-wall *burh* or fortified enclosure and a royal palace of timber (built for Edwin of Northumbria). Throughout the period timber was the chief material for less important buildings, though all have perished except the church at Greensted (Essex), which shows the upright, split-log technique used for wall construction.

Through contact with the Rhineland the Saxons acquired a stone technique. Writers in the eighth century mention quite large buildings, though they had a tendency to exaggerate and surviving examples are certainly small.

The earliest stone buildings were churches erected in the seventh century after the conversion that followed St Augustine's mission in 597. A group of Roman-style churches, in brick, with naves, apsidal chancels, narthexes and *portici* (porches used as side chapels) was built in Kent. A representative example is St Pancras at Canterbury.

A north-eastern group was of stone with long, high, narrow naves, tall elevations and towers and square-ended chancels of Celtic influence. Monkwearmouth is a good example of this second group, with a unique, above-ground groined vault in the tower porch. (There are several Saxon crypts.) This is the first time that the square-ended chancel is met in England, a feature associated with the Celtic Church and one that was adopted for most English Gothic churches after becoming absorbed into the tradition.

Besides these smaller churches there must have been some larger ones of the basilica type but the only one extant is at Brixworth in Northamptonshire. This is a simplified early Christian basilica consisting of nave, aisles, clerestory and apsidal east end, constructed of Roman brick with Roman arcades.

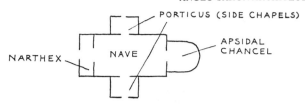

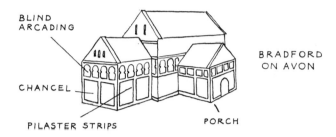

ANGLO-SAXON CHURCHES

The carved ornament of early Saxon churches is sparse but boldly executed in the manner of the seventh-century high crosses, and like them it combines Celtic interlacing with Mediterranean motifs such as vine and ivy scroll with animals and figures, as can be seen at Ruthwell and Easby.

From the ninth century until the Conquest (the period of the supremacy of Wessex and of the Viking invasions) later Saxon work was influenced from abroad. It brought from the Rhineland, for example, the double cross plan of some of the major churches now destroyed and also the helm-shaped roof. But in general churches continued to be small with elementary compartment-like plans, though some had porches that became incipient transepts giving a cruciform effect. The square east end was now definitely preferred to the apse.

Workmanship continued to be rather rustic but was sound enough, as can be seen today. High nave walls were essayed and it is remarkable what the tenth- and eleventh-century Saxons were able to achieve in the way of monumental dignity in spite of the smallness of scale.

Piers were short and stumpy with square capitals. Vaults were simple, either barrel or groined. Windows were small and round or triangular-headed, with narrow apertures but wide internal splays

INTERNAL SPLAY

BALUSTER SHAFT

QUOINS

QUOINS

FIVE LIGHT BELFRY WINDOW

LONG & SHORT WORK

MEGALITHIC

LONG & SHORT WORK

LATTICE WORK

PILASTER STRIPS

DOORWAY

BLIND ARCADING

HELM FORM FROM RHINELAND

SOMPTING

ENRICHED TOWER
EARLS
BARTON

ANGLO-SAXON FEATURES

to admit the maximum light. Late Saxon belfry windows often had baluster shafts. There was no glazing and shutters kept the weather out. Doorways were also round-headed and some in the eleventh century had carved tympana.

Emphasising the angles of walls or articulating them at intervals were pilaster strips, which may also have served as vertical bonding courses in the rubble or ragstone walls. Another wall feature was blind arcading. Quoins, either megalithic or long and short work, strengthened and decorated the angles. Arches were usually left plain, though a few were given simple but massive mouldings. By the eleventh century western and central towers were common. They were without buttresses and frequently terminated in the helm form of roof.

There was less carved ornament and it was not as successful. The total effect of the abstract patterning, however, was often quite rich, as can be seen from the tower at Earls Barton.

Strictly speaking there were no Saxon castles, for the *burh* was essentially the community defence and not the private fortress of later times. The Saxon thane lived in a single hall which served as a manor house. This must have been made chiefly of timber, the roof supported by walls and wooden posts. Windows were small, again for practical reasons, and the communal life of the hall was orientated on the central hearth, the smoke from which escaped through a louvre in the roof overhead. The peasants continued to live in huts that were frameworks of wood turfed or thatched.

Anglo-Norman architecture

Anglo-Norman was another form of Romanesque architecture, superior in many ways to Anglo-Saxon. It began even before the Conquest, for Edward the Confessor adopted this style for the rebuilding of Westminster Abbey in grander, more spacious manner.

Anglo-Norman is a style with breadth and a sense of power. Its blunt, massive forms are aesthetically successful and exhibit a unity of design hitherto somewhat lacking in native work. Technically also it shows an advance on Anglo-Saxon architecture, for though most of the craftsmen must have been Saxon, the architects and master-masons were often brought across from Normandy.

The pre-eminent building type was the church. Anglo-Norman parish churches resemble their Saxon predecessors since they are usually aisle-less and compartmental in plan (though larger) and originally consisted of up to four cells with an apsidal end.

Larger churches display a more complex type of plan, generally cruciform with developed transepts to increase accommodation and give light and tower abutment. Some are aisled basilicas of three storeys, a triforium or blindstorey appearing between the nave arcade and the clerestory, at the level of the aisle roof. The arcades themselves have round arches resting on massive cylindrical, polygonal or compound piers. Vaults are either of the barrel or groined quadripartite types. In some churches the nave is barrel-vaulted with cross vaults over the aisles, as can be seen in the remarkably little altered eleventh-century interior of St John's Chapel in the Tower of London. Larger spans had timber ceilings, until in the late twelfth century at Durham Cathedral (that

CUSHION   COMPOUND   SCALLOPED   POLYGONAL

NORMAN PIERS & CAPITALS

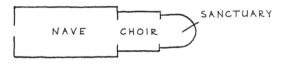

SMALLER NORMAN CHURCH
THREE CELL TYPE

magnificent culmination of Anglo-Norman effort) the problem was solved by the construction of the first ribbed high vault in Europe, abutted by arches concealed under the aisle roofs. Such a high vault was useful because of the added protection it gave to the church against fire, and it marked an important step in the transition to the Gothic style by the way it unified the bays more emphatically. The suggestion that the ribs were a purely technical device to save stone is discredited by the fact that here the panels of the web are no lighter than in corresponding groined vaults.

Broad, flat buttresses mark the bay divisions externally but are not really required for abutment on account of the thickness and strength of the walls. Openings are round-headed, some recessed in 'orders' with nook shafts. Windows are commonly of one large single light flanked by blind arcading. The towers of larger churches, mostly rebuilt during the Norman period, were placed centrally and were squat and massive in appearance. Some churches had two-tower west façades, a key element in Romanesque and Gothic that originated at Strasbourg in 1015 and was imported here from Normandy. Pyramidal roofs were usual.

Two phases can be distinguished in Anglo-Norman architecture. That of the eleventh century was plain with meagre decoration, such as simple mouldings and crocket foliage on the capitals, and favoured a continental east end either of the parallel-apse or chevet type. The twelfth-century phase, called High Romanesque, is characterised by much rich decoration, notably the boldly executed designs of chevron, cable and beak head (the latter an interesting motif of Scandinavian origin). West fronts are elaborate, as at Castle Acre Priory, and doorways particularly lavishly decorated with scrollwork filled with animals and figures and perhaps adorned with a carved tympanum, as at Malmesbury Abbey. Walls are embellished with blind arcading, often interlaced, and pier capitals enriched with carving.

In High Romanesque can be detected what were to become three of the favourite elements of Gothic architecture: the square east end of the native type, once again reverted to at Southwell Minster; the double transept which began with the extension at

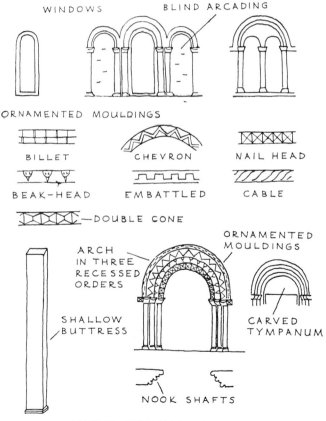

WINDOWS   BLIND ARCADING

ORNAMENTED MOULDINGS

BILLET   CHEVRON   NAIL HEAD

BEAK-HEAD   EMBATTLED   CABLE

—DOUBLE CONE

ARCH IN THREE RECESSED ORDERS

ORNAMENTED MOULDINGS

SHALLOW BUTTRESS

CARVED TYMPANUM

NOOK SHAFTS

ANGLO-NORMAN FEATURES

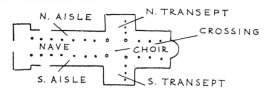

DURHAM CATHEDRAL

SECTION OF AISLED BASILICAN CHURCH

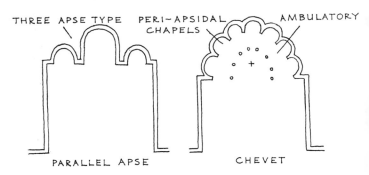

11th. CENT. NORMAN EAST ENDS

Canterbury; and the Lady chapel added to the east end to serve the growing cult of the Virgin Mary.

The castle was the private stronghold of the lord or magnate and also his manor house, where he administered local government and justice and dispensed hospitality.

The first Norman castles in England were small 'motte and bailey' structures of earth and timber. A classic example of this type can still be traced at Berkhamsted. Such a castle was relatively easy to erect with speed and with non-specialist forced labour, but by the mid twelfth century its materials were being

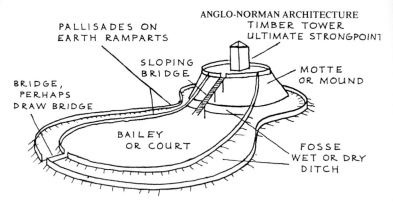

PALLISADES ON
EARTH RAMPARTS

ANGLO-NORMAN ARCHITECTURE
TIMBER TOWER
ULTIMATE STRONGPOINT

SLOPING
BRIDGE

MOTTE
OR MOUND

BRIDGE,
PERHAPS
DRAW BRIDGE

BAILEY
OR COURT

FOSSE
WET OR DRY
DITCH

MOTTE & BAILEY CASTLE : 11th. & 12th. CENT.

translated into stonework. The timber tower, the ultimate
strongpoint, became the stone keep or *donjon,* and the stockaded
ramparts a stone curtain wall. Thus the two original elements of
defence are still preserved in the keep and bailey castle, as at
Richmond (N. Yorks). Some had in addition a square or twin-
towered gatehouse to defend the approach, and stone buildings in
the bailey, like the late eleventh-century aisled hall at Richmond.

Keeps became quite elaborate. At first they were square in plan,
massive and thick-walled, and because of their great weight less
often raised on a mound of earth. Sometimes there was a splayed
plinth to protect the base and strengthen it. The usual practice was
to divide the structure vertically into four storeys. The basement,

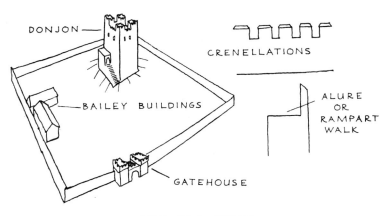

DONJON

CRENELLATIONS

BAILEY BUILDINGS

ALURE
OR
RAMPART
WALK

GATEHOUSE

MID 12th. CENT.

ANGLO-NORMAN ARCHITECTURE

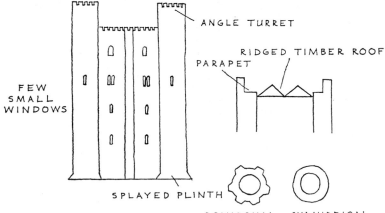

FEW SMALL WINDOWS

ANGLE TURRET

RIDGED TIMBER ROOF

PARAPET

SPLAYED PLINTH

POLYGONAL   CYLINDRICAL

DEEP SPLAYS TO OPENINGS

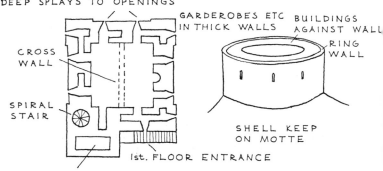

CROSS WALL

SPIRAL STAIR

FOREBUILDING

GARDEROBES ETC IN THICK WALLS

BUILDINGS AGAINST WALL

RING WALL

SHELL KEEP ON MOTTE

1st. FLOOR ENTRANCE

12th CENTURY CASTLE KEEPS

ground floor or undercroft was vaulted with stone and served for storage. Above this the first floor lodged the garrison, the second served as the great hall and the third contained the private apartments of the lord, such as the solar. The upper floors were equipped with fireplaces but otherwise centrally placed braziers were used. There were a few small windows. A double-ridged timber roof completed the building, placed below parapet level to preserve it from exposure and to assist fire control. The plan was often divided by a lateral cross wall to strengthen the structure of the keep and to facilitate flooring and roofing. The vise or solid newel spiral staircase (which was to continue as the universal type of staircase throughout the Gothic period which followed) was a utilitarian feature tucked away in one of the four angle turrets. Garderobes were set in the thickness of the wall.

Entrance to the keep was at first-floor level up a flight of steps at the side of the keep, leading to a forebuilding which protected the castle door. In this way attackers exposed their flank and a direct assault on the keep was impossible. Some keeps had a chapel in the upper part of the forebuilding.

The square keep or *donjon* is by far the most usual twelfth-century type, but there were some shell keeps (e.g. Windsor, built on a motte) where buildings were placed against a ring wall. In the later part of the century these began to be superseded by round keeps (a crusader fashion brought from the Near East), which were less vulnerable since the angles of the square keep were eliminated. There are also some polygonal examples.

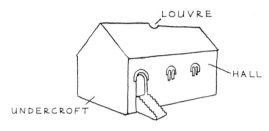

STONE BUILT NORMAN MANOR HOUSE

Very few Norman domestic buildings survive, but they probably resembled the domestic buildings of the twelfth-century monasteries, with or without aisles. For instance, Boothby Pagnell is a simple, rectangular, stone manor house consisting of a common hall with a solar at one end and kitchens at the other, all raised upon an undercroft. It is probable that added protection was given by surrounding the hall with a moat or wall.

The type of masonry used at this time continued into the earlier part of the next period. Probably owing to the relative shortage of skilled stone cutters, it consisted chiefly of roughly shaped or uncut rubble stones mixed with mortar to produce a kind of concrete and was finally faced with well-cut stone. Arches, mouldings, shafts, ribs and carving were all executed in cut stone. Herringbone work is an occasional feature of the eleventh century, both Saxon and Norman.

3. Gothic

The sources of the Gothic style were certain great churches of the Ile de France and the later Cistercian abbeys of Burgundy. It emerged in England towards the end of the twelfth century and prevailed for the next 350 years. Essentially it was a new synthesis of existing features for the realisation of original technical and aesthetic aims.

First, the pointed arch made possible the construction of rectangular vaults that were stable, thus doubling the amount of support for the high vault. At the same time ribs concentrated the vault thrusts and directed them to particular points. Pointed arches and ribs together created the Gothic cross vault.

Flying buttresses or, more commonly in England, half arches concealed under the aisle roofs may be seen conducting the thrust of the high vault over the aisles to vertical wall buttresses, which

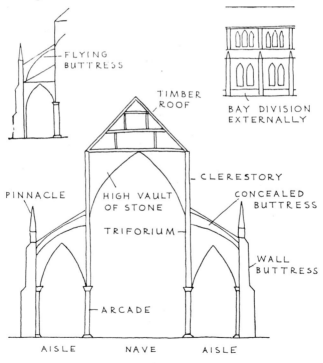

FLYING BUTTRESS

TIMBER ROOF

BAY DIVISION EXTERNALLY

CLERESTORY

PINNACLE

HIGH VAULT OF STONE

CONCEALED BUTTRESS

TRIFORIUM

WALL BUTTRESS

ARCADE

AISLE   NAVE   AISLE

then direct it to the ground. This concentration of thrusts along certain lines and the bringing down of the weight of the building to isolated points allow the walls to be opened up by large windows, which are such a characteristic feature of Gothic.

The Gothic system may therefore be seen as an organic one, in which stability is achieved not by great masses of masonry as in Romanesque but by a tense balance of opposing forces that is both ingenious and logical. In other respects, however, its principal structures — the great churches — carry on the Romanesque tradition of the staggered basilican elevation and cruciform plan, sometimes with Romanesque eastern transepts.

One transition from Romanesque to Gothic has been noted in the high vault at Durham, but the first consistently Gothic buildings in England were the Cistercian abbeys of the north (Roche, 1165) and the rebuilding of the choir of Canterbury Cathedral, also in the late twelfth century.

It is still useful to adopt Rickman's early nineteenth-century classification of English Gothic into Early English, Decorated and Perpendicular, corresponding roughly to the thirteenth, fourteenth and fifteenth centuries, though the style is really a continuously evolving one and most buildings are composite.

Early English (thirteenth century)

The first flowering of Gothic is noticeably lighter than the preceding Romanesque. It emphasises the vertical and its general lines are clean and crisp. Its feeling is one of austere aspiration.

Arcades are pointed and slender, the piers formed of clustered shafts, often detached and of marble, but later merged with the main column. Capitals are adorned with stylised foliage and outlines are emphasised with bold mouldings and deep hollows, some bearing 'dogtooth' decoration. Other ornaments are diaper patterns and arcading on walls. Vaults are ribbed but relatively simple in form (e.g. quadripartite); wall buttresses project boldly, often receding in stages with niches, offsets and gablets. Fenestration is typically in pairs or groups of lancet windows united by a dripstone. Later the spandrels were pierced to give plate tracery which in turn developed into geometrical bar tracery. Roofs are high-pitched and towers finished with a spire of stone or timber, often with 'broaches' to make the transition from four-sided tower to octagonal spire.

The keep and bailey castle continued to be built in this period but the special innovation of the thirteenth century was the concentric castle, in which the keep had become redundant owing to the improvement of bailey defences by the addition of mural towers. The type can be traced back through the Crusades and the Turks to the military architecture of Rome. In its latest form it is an organic system of concentric curtain walls, quadrangular or polygonal in plan and carefully exploiting the contours of the site, strengthened at intervals by towers.

These towers were at first square but later polygonal and circular. Though they projected to command the face of the curtain they were often flush inside. Their bases were given a batter or spurred to strengthen them. Inside were guard rooms and apartments.

The principal defensive parts of the concentric castles were the gatehouses, twin-towered in the twelfth and early thirteenth centuries but later joined above the gate to make a single massive structure over a narrow entrance passage, with portcullis and machicolations (apertures in a corbelled parapet) above. Unlike the keep they were not entirely defensive, being thrust forward in a more aggressive manner. Features playing a similar role were posterns and barbicans. Crenellation was further improved in the thirteenth and fourteenth centuries: merlons were narrowed, embrasures and loops multiplied and stone machicolations evolved from overhanging timber hoarding. Though the concentric castle is essentially a functional design its frequent symmetry and geometrical forms often endow it with a remarkable aesthetic quality, as at Harlech.

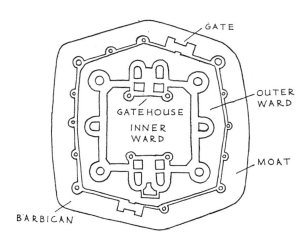

BEAUMARIS 1295

Some examples of planned fortified towns of this period still survive, such as Flint with its chequer-board plan.

The thirteenth-century manor house was still basically a hall

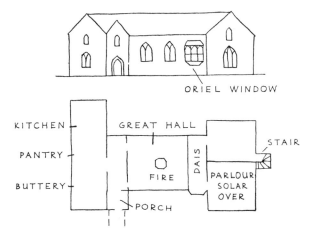

serving as the chief living-room and general dormitory, but more rooms began to be added — perhaps a parlour with solar above at the upper end, and a kitchen, buttery, pantry and larder at the lower. Licences to crenellate permitted fortification, such as the tower at Stokesay. Open timber roofs were still the rule but glass, hooded wall fireplaces and chimneys began to make their appearance instead of shutters and louvres.

Decorated (fourteenth century)

This phase of Gothic began with Henry III's sumptuous reconstruction of Westminster Abbey. It is characterised, as its name suggests, by rich decoration but also by new effects of light and shade, surface movement and space, such as the lantern tower (the octagon) that 'floats' over the crossing at Ely. The ogee arch is typical in windows and canopies.

Arcades are now wider, piers taller and more slender, with all lesser shafts engaged. Vaults are composed in elaborate web-like patterns by the addition of extra ribs such as tiercerons and non-structural liernes with decorative bosses at the intersections. Buttresses are more varied and usually enriched with ogee forms and other ornament. Walls are thinner and into them are introduced larger, broader windows with curvilinear bar tracery, a Gothic invention, making flowing, organic patterns based on ogee curves, as at Selby Abbey. Their stained glass is more translucent and freer in design. Roofs are still high-pitched but the broach spire is replaced by one that is more slender and graceful, springing from within a parapet and ornamented with angle pinnacles, crockets, spirelights and bands of incised quatrefoil.

RIBBED VAULT

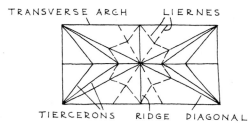

TRANSVERSE ARCH   LIERNES

TIERCERONS   RIDGE   DIAGONAL

Towers show a decorative use of angle buttresses and contrasts between plain and enriched surfaces, as on the west front of York Minster. Wave-like and ogee mouldings are broader and shallower than Early English ones and appear for the first time on the chamfer plane. Decorated ornament is profuse and flowing, based on the naturalistic foliage of ivy, oak and vine. Ball flower is a typical motif and niches are common.

From the late fourteenth century the castle declined in importance with the decay of feudalism, the increase in the central power of the monarchy, the changes in social life and the development of field armies and gunpowder. In the years between 1350 and 1550 domestic amenities grew at the expense of defences until in late Tudor times the castle merged with the manor house. The fourteenth-century quadrangular castle without curtain walls

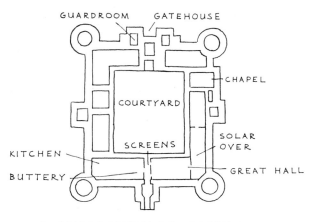

A QUADRANGULAR CASTLE
BODIAM CASTLE 1385

shows this transition, as at Bolton (N. Yorks) and Lumley (Durham), where residential buildings are compactly disposed round a courtyard and equipped with angle tower to create a building that is both fortress and residence. On the Scottish border the pele towers, set in walled courtyards (barmkins), still preserve the earlier keep and bailey tradition.

In fourteenth-century manor houses like Penshurst Place, often the country retreats of the new city merchants, the hall remains the centre, but screens, with minstrels' gallery above, shut out the offices, and windows are larger with a bay or oriel window at the high-table end. The buildings, sometimes including a chapel, are roofed separately, entered from the outside, and generally arranged round a quadrangular court with a fortified gatehouse opposite the entrance to the hall. Their total effect is asymmetrical and picturesque. Like the castles, the manor houses of this period are often moated.

Perpendicular (fifteenth century)

Perpendicular is a form of late Gothic architecture peculiar to England: a kind of national medieval style. It is a rather materialistic version, its vertical and horizontal emphases giving it a characteristic squareness of outline. The earliest Perpendicular work is actually of the fourteenth century and can be seen in Gloucester Cathedral choir and the nave of Canterbury rebuilt by the famous Henry Yevele. The first of these has the broad-arched windows with rectilinear network of glazed panels, the 'applied' vault ribs and the stonework panelling that are typical Perpendicular features; the second shows the Perpendicular tendency to heighten both aisles and nave arcades, often at the expense of the triforium, to create a two-storeyed building in which the internal spaces merge and thereby achieve a greater unity.

Though arcades are high their arches are now lower and broader, the mouldings often continuing down the piers since the capitals almost disappear or are replaced by horizontal moulding. Engaged pier shafts almost merge and become like mouldings. Carrying on the Decorated trend of elaboration, vault ribs multiply further into complicated patterns of non-structural features, often merely carved on the vault surface. These rich lierne stellar designs continue, therefore, together with new types developed from them: the fan vault — appearing first in the Severn Valley — and its variant the pendant vault. All have a flatter curvature to accord with the lower arches, the broad windows and the stone panelled walls, so that the whole impression is a remarkably unified one.

Buttresses are structurally important, on account of the wider windows and more slender piers, and they often end in pinnacles.

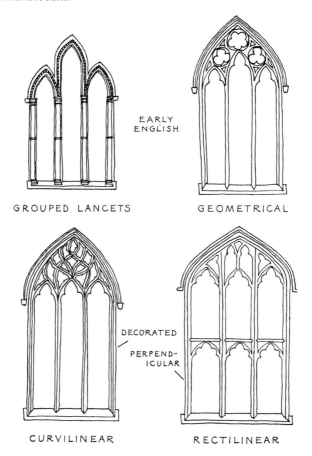

EARLY
ENGLISH

GROUPED LANCETS

GEOMETRICAL

DECORATED

PERPEND-
ICULAR

CURVILINEAR

RECTILINEAR

The typical Perpendicular window has a low arch, transoms, 'gridiron' tracery and less opaque pictorial glazing. Roofs are low-pitched, lead being preferred to tiles, and they are often provided with battlemented parapets, usually panelled or pierced.

The tower is a special late Gothic feature and many were added during this period of extension. There are even recognisable regional 'schools' of design like those of Somerset and East Anglia. Most have 'crowns'; some are 'lanterns' lighting the crossing (a Romanesque motif); some have an octagonal lantern on top; and a few continue to support spires of the Decorated type.

GOTHIC PIERS

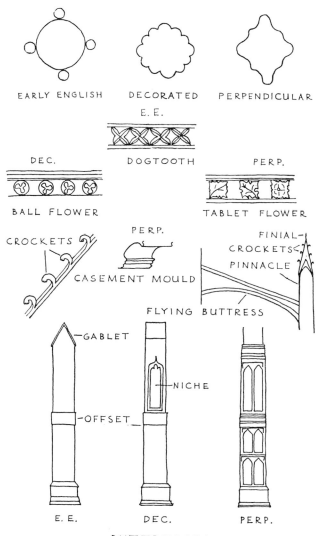

EARLY ENGLISH   DECORATED   PERPENDICULAR

E. E.

DEC.   DOGTOOTH   PERP.

BALL FLOWER   TABLET FLOWER

CROCKETS   PERP.   FINIAL

CROCKETS

PINNACLE

CASEMENT MOULD

FLYING BUTTRESS

GABLET

NICHE

OFFSET

E. E.   DEC.   PERP.

BUTTRESSES

29

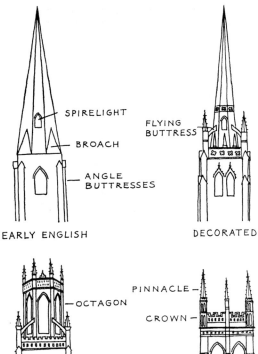

PERPENDICULAR

SPIRELIGHT

BROACH

FLYING
BUTTRESS

ANGLE
BUTTRESSES

EARLY ENGLISH

DECORATED

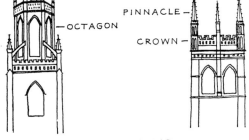

OCTAGON

PINNACLE —

CROWN —

PERPENDICULAR

GOTHIC TOWERS & SPIRES

Mouldings are shallow, lean, wiry and cut on the chamfer. The 'casement' type is common. Ornament includes the repeated shallow rectilinear panelling, framing cusped arches (already referred to) and also heraldic emblems, miniature battlements, Tudor roses and fleurs-de-lis. Generally it is harsher and more geometrical than Decorated ornament.

Castles and manor houses like Haddon Hall and Great Chalfield followed fourteenth-century trends, arranged round courtyards with the addition of more space, bedrooms and supplementary offices. In the countryside more small halls appeared for prosperous wool farmers and merchants, whose wealth financed the rebuilding of parish churches and the erection of town and guild halls, markets, inns, schools, colleges, tithe barns, dovecotes and bridges.

Materials varied from region to region: sandstone in the north and west, limestone along the Jurassic outcrop, brick and flintwork in East Anglia, and timber framing everywhere that wood was plentiful and stone scarce.

Timber roofs

Timber roofs, open from below in unvaulted buildings, are among the many interesting features of Gothic construction. They culminate in the elaborate superstructures that were a special English achievement of the late middle ages.

The earliest type was the simple tie-beam designed to prevent

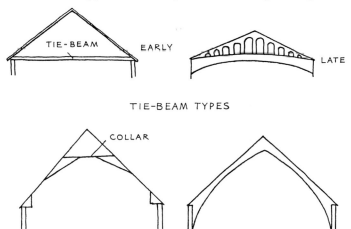

TIE-BEAM   EARLY   LATE

TIE-BEAM TYPES

COLLAR

TRUSSED RAFTER   ARCH-BRACED

the roof from spreading. Probably the only Norman type of roof, it was in common use for smaller buildings throughout the Gothic period. There were many variations, however. For example, in the Perpendicular phase the low-pitched roof often rested directly on a slightly curved tie-beam.

In the mid thirteenth century new types began to emerge, such as the trussed rafter with its timbers joined by collars stiffened by braces, thus giving greater height. Another type was the arch-braced roof where curved timbers spring from the upper parts of the walls. But the most splendid medieval timber roofs are the hammer-beams, usually fifteenth-century, though that of Westminster Hall by Hugh Herland dates from the late four-teenth. This is a development of earlier types, its curved timbers springing from brackets projecting from the walls with sup-plementary buttresses outside to help divert the thrust earthwards. No longer need a hall be aisled, for a much wider span is possible by this ingenious arrangement. The most inventive and decorative

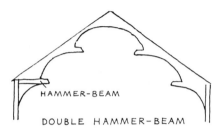

HAMMER-BEAM

DOUBLE HAMMER-BEAM

examples are those of the East Anglian churches. Coloured, gilded and combined with large clerestory windows, they give a spacious, lantern-like effect. March (Cambs) has a splendid double ham-mer-beam with angels hovering overhead. It is a feature which often compensates for the prosaic uniformity of some Per-pendicular interiors.

Roof covering consisted of stone tiles, tiles or wood shingles in the earlier period, with lead later becoming more usual on roofs of lower pitch.

English medieval architecture is noted for the number of domestic and administrative buildings which survive from the great religious establishments and among these the polygonal chapter houses like Lincoln and York are of outstanding merit and unique to England.

Gothic church plans

Gothic church planning reflects very closely the changing needs of the middle ages. Twelfth-century parish churches were aisled or unaisled, with or without transepts. But as the population ex-panded they grew piecemeal by the addition of aisles or the lengthening of chancels. South porches were common throughout the period. The fourteenth and fifteenth centuries brought much remodelling that resulted in lighter and more spacious aisles, and the cruciform transeptal type became less usual until in the later fifteenth and early sixteenth centuries there was a reversion to the undivided plan, following the example of the friars' preaching hall. This was first achieved by carrying forward the aisles to the

1. Bath, Avon: the reconstructed remains of the ancient lead-lined baths of the Roman Aquae Sulis at the centre of the eighteenth-century Georgian spa.
2. Chesters, Northumberland: the bath house of the Roman fort of Cilurnum had an elaborate system of hot and cold rooms.

3. All Saints church, Brixworth, Northamptonshire, formerly an aisled basilica. The major monument of seventh-century Saxon England. The arches of Roman brick lack technical expertise.

4. *Castle Acre Priory, Norfolk: twelfth-century blind arcading on the west front of the church of this Cluniac foundation.*

5. *St Albans Cathedral, Hertfordshire: the long Gothic nave of the Benedictine abbey hides a plain Romanesque core, built, like the severe central tower, of bricks from Verulamium.*

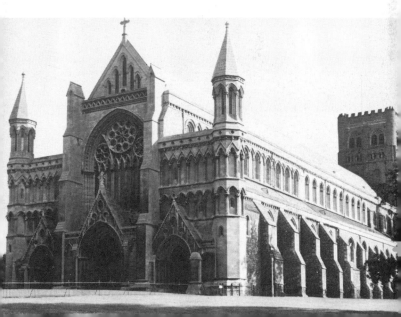

6. Gloucester Cathedral: massive Anglo-Norman arcades support a lighter Early English rib vault. Beyond the pulpitum is the more complex work of the fourteenth-century choir.

7. Framlingham Castle, Suffolk: a twelfth-century curtain-wall castle with projecting mural towers. The construction in flint is due to the absence of good stone locally.

8. Stokesay Castle, Salop: a thirteenth-century fortified manor house, the product of a 'licence to crenellate' and the insecurity of life on the Welsh March.

9. *Rievaulx Abbey, North Yorkshire: the austere grandeur of the moulded forms of Early English Gothic; a monument to the Cistercian colonisation of the northern wastes.*

10. *Ely Cathedral, Cambridgeshire: this view of the south transept shows the composite character of much Gothic (cf window forms). The octagon over the crossing is timber sheathed in lead.*

11. St Mary's church, Fairford, Gloucestershire: a splendid fifteenth-century Cotswold wool church of oolitic limestone with a rare set of surviving medieval stained glass windows.

12. Wells Cathedral, Somerset: the superb and richly sculptured early Gothic west front, broad and screen-like. The towers are of a later date.

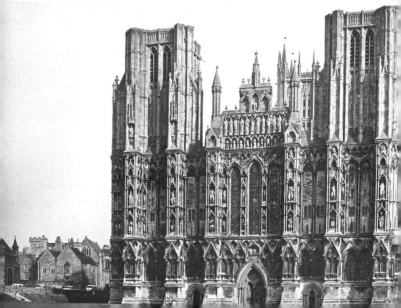

13. York Minster: the two-towered west front on a huge scale features effective contrasts between plain surfaces and elaborately traceried windows.

14. The Beauchamp Chapel, St Mary's church, Warwick: a small but sumptuous late Gothic interior with fan vaulting and typical Perpendicular windows with strongly marked verticals.

15. *Boston Stump, Lincolnshire: the tower of St Botolph's church expresses both a transcendent faith and the civic pride of an important medieval seaport.*

16. *Lavenham, Suffolk: a well preserved late medieval wool town, rich in timber-framed and plastered vernacular like the Wool Hall and the Guildhall.*

17. *The George Inn, Norton St Philip, Somerset: one of the few remaining medieval inns. Note the use of materials and the jettied (overhanging) storeys.*

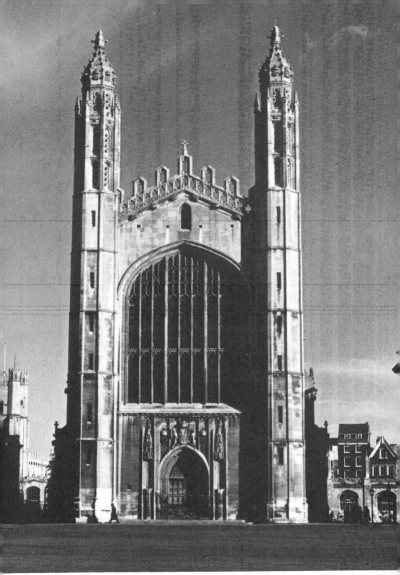

18. King's College Chapel, Cambridge: England in the reign of Henry VII was still committed to late Gothic, though the Renaissance had matured in Italy by this time.

19. Layer Marney Towers, Essex, a brick-built Tudor house, shows how the gatehouse had become ornamental. The Renaissance motifs in terracotta are probably by Italian craftsmen.

20. Hayes Barton, East Budleigh, Devon: a sixteenth-century E-plan house, the birthplace of Raleigh, though humbly constructed of ancient cob (unbaked earth) and thatched.

21. Lord Leycester's Hospital, Warwick: Elizabethan almshouses with a great hall, valued by English taste for picturesque rather than architectural qualities.

22. Longleat House, Wiltshire: a symmetrical, finely articulated early Renaissance design in Bath stone, probably the best of the Elizabethan 'prodigy' houses.

23. Kirby Hall, Northamptonshire: the ruined courtyard. It began as an Elizabethan house and received sophisticated additions with contemporary French motifs.

24. Sudbury Hall, Derbyshire: built progressively through the seventeenth century. The patterned brickwork is characteristic of the earlier period; the roof with dormers and massive chimney stacks is later.

length of the chancel, as in certain East Anglian churches; then in larger ones by designing aisled halls, as distinct from basilicas (e.g. Bristol); and lastly by unaisled halls as at King's College Chapel, Cambridge.

The typical English Gothic cathedral has a spread-out, ramifying plan with large transepts, often double. This results in a group composition that requires a central tower to give it unity. East ends are square and of two types. One, the south-west

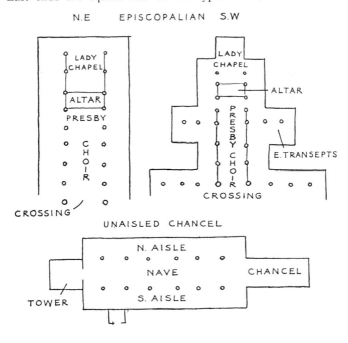

episcopalian (e.g. Salisbury), has a projecting chapel lower than the choir which combines with the double transepts to create a grouped composition. The other, the north-east episcopalian (e.g. York), is an aisled parallelogram with a towering monumental façade — the definitive east end of the English cathedral. Chapter houses are a distinctive national feature and there are many interesting versions, as at Wells and Westminster.

The great Gothic churches afford a good example of how

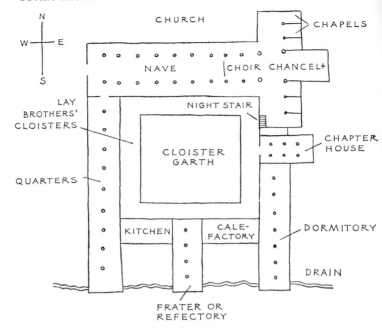

CISTERCIAN MONASTERY

buildings express the culture and values of their time, for they are the embodiment of the religious spirit of the middle ages. The plan expresses the ritual of the Church. There is singleness of purpose in the uninterrupted progress of the arcades towards the high altar and aspiration in the soaring verticals of piers, buttresses, pinnacles and towers.

Another expression of the medieval religious spirit was withdrawal from the world, a recognised ideal that gave rise to monastic communities, either ascetic like the Cistercians, who farmed in remote places, or scholarly and learned like the more aristocratic Benedictines, many of whose churches became cathedrals.

These settlements were centred round a great church, usually sited on the north to give shelter to the conventual buildings. The processional entrance was in the west end of the nave, to which the public was confined by screens. But there was another door in the south transept. The chapter house, where the business and discipline of the community were carried on, lay off the east cloister, on the same side as the monks' day room, with dorter over. The refectory was usually along the south cloister, away from the church, and was arranged like a secular hall but equipped with a pulpit or reading desk. Adjacent were the kitchens and *calefactory* (warming room for recreation). The lay brothers' quarters were on the west side of the garth and one cloister was usually furnished with carrels for study.

Detached from this well-balanced and orderly main group lay the abbot's lodging, the guesthouse, the infirmary with herb garden, servants' hall and kitchen, granary, brewhouse, bakery, almonry, workshop, mill, fishpool and all the other appurtenances of a self-contained community, economic as well as spiritual.

Medieval building industry

The amount of medieval building carried out in relation to the population of from two to four millions is astonishing and could only have been possible with a highly organised and competent industry. Some Romanesque clerics had architectural knowledge, but by Gothic times there was a complete lay organisation and the architect was the 'master of works', usually a mason like William of Sens, who rebuilt Canterbury. Under him were the master craftsmen in charge of their various departments. From the thirteenth century the names of architects began to be recorded when their status became recognised. Plans were merely diagrammatic, since drawing technique was very elementary, and the tools of their workmen untempered and inferior. The labour force consisted of large numbers of skilled itinerants, whose wages accounted for two-thirds of the building costs. They included rough masons, free masons, carpenters, smiths, plasterers, glaziers, tilers, paviers, hodmen, clerks, woodmen, sawyers, limeworkers, miners and carters together with impressed labour as required. At Beaumaris Castle there were four hundred masons, thirty smiths and carpenters, two hundred carters and a thousand unskilled labourers. At Durham 1500 tons (1524t) of masonry were used in five years. These materials either came from local quarries and forests or were transported by water, some from as far away as Caen in Normandy.

Tudor (early sixteenth century)

Tudor architecture is really the last phase of Gothic. It is essentially Perpendicular with a few graftings of the new Renaissance influence from Italy. The mullioned windows, the flattened four-centred arches of the wide arcades, the piers and vaulting types are all Perpendicular, though there is a further evolution of fan vaulting into 'pendant vaulting' where the main vault springs from pendant voussoirs of the transverse arches and

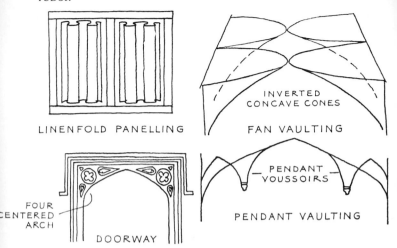

LINENFOLD PANELLING

INVERTED
CONCAVE CONES

FAN VAULTING

FOUR
CENTERED
ARCH

DOORWAY

PENDANT
VOUSSOIRS

PENDANT VAULTING

not from the side walls, so that it appears to be suspended overhead. The vault of Henry VII's chapel at Westminster is an example of this.

The Renaissance element is chiefly confined to a few superficial decorative forms of Italianate ornament executed by foreign craftsmen. Such are Henry VII's tomb by Torrigiano, the stalls at King's College, Cambridge, and the *amorini* and terracotta roundels with Roman emperors' heads at Hampton Court Palace.

In 1538 Henry VIII broke with Rome and the Reformation began. Monastic establishments were dissolved and their estates sold to eager buyers, merchants who built for themselves new country houses. The middle ages had provided England with a rich dower of ecclesiastical buildings and now, after the Reformation, the church as the principal architectural type was to give way to the country mansion, which was dominant until the nineteenth century.

Typical Tudor country houses are of two kinds: either on the old quadrangular plan with a gatehouse, or the newer type consisting of a rectangular block to which are attached short, compact wings and often a projecting central porch. As yet there is no internal symmetry, but there is a tendency to greater symmetry in the elevations — no doubt an indirect classical Renaissance influence. Once more the number of rooms increases with the addition of summer and winter parlours, study and bedrooms, though the latter are still 'thoroughfare' rooms. For the first time 'state rooms' appear, like the great chamber and the dining chamber. But the basic arrangement of a great hall with service rooms at one end and private apartments at the other is still a medieval conception.

The individual features of these houses are also Gothic — for example the square-headed windows with mullions and transoms and sharply pitched roofs and gables. Brick was being more widely used now and bay and oriel windows became more common. Tall and elaborate chimneys are notable external features resulting from the use of coal, functional yet ornamental.

Internally there are wall fireplaces with rich overmantels, linenfold panelling and relief plasterwork that finds its highest expression in the decorative ceilings of the period, replete with ribs, vine trails and pendants. All these speak of an improved standard of material comfort.

Some Tudor houses like Layer Marney and Coughton Court retained the separate gateway — perhaps with octagonal towers, turrets and battlements — though it was no longer intended for anything but display.

BARRINGTON COURT 1518

Timber framing

Though doubtless in stone districts some of the smaller houses of the middle ages and Tudor times were of simple stone construction, the majority were primitive timber-framed buildings of the 'cruck' or 'crick' type. These were built in 'bays' or units of 16 feet (4.88m). Pairs of crucks were obtained by splitting timbers that were naturally curved, and across two or more of these pairs was placed a ridge pole. The timbers were roughly squared with an adze and pegged together. Walls were filled with 'wattle and daub' (hazel or willow twigs woven into hurdles, daubed with clay and chopped straw, and coated with lime plaster). The roof was thatched with straw or reeds.

Ties were used to prevent the crucks from spreading and it was found that by extending the ties outwards to posts carrying horizontal 'pans' vertical walls could be raised, giving more height.

From these earlier examples developed the more ambitious 'post

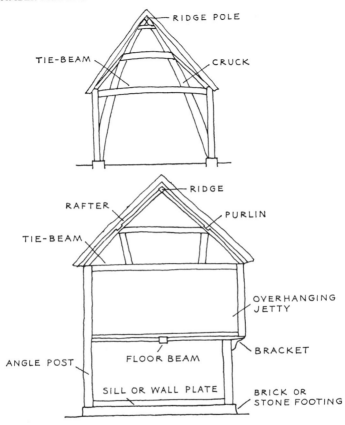

RIDGE POLE

TIE-BEAM

CRUCK

RIDGE

RAFTER

PURLIN

TIE-BEAM

OVERHANGING
JETTY

BRACKET

ANGLE POST

FLOOR BEAM

SILL OR WALL PLATE

BRICK OR
STONE FOOTING

and truss' timber-framed houses of the fifteenth and sixteenth centuries, with their rectangular wall-frames supporting proper roof-trusses. These were the yeomen's houses in the country, merchants' town houses, exchanges, guild and market halls erected anywhere that stone was scarce. Timbers were prepared before being brought to the site and were assembled by being pegged together on stone footings. Again the spaces were filled with wattle and daub or, in some later instances, brickwork 'nogging', often of the herringbone type. Houses were of several storeys, with earlier examples jettied (i.e. overhanging). In East Anglia the wood framing was often plastered over and decorated with moulded designs called pargeting.

4. Renaissance

The Renaissance was the rebirth of Classical culture, when the more circumscribed medieval ways of life and thought were replaced by the rediscovered philosophy and art of ancient Greece and Rome, bringing a new emphasis on humanism, reason and objective inquiry. The movement came to England first through literature, then the visual arts and lastly architecture. It began in Italy in the fifteenth century but took over a hundred years to influence architecture in England, at first making its way tentatively in the decorative motifs, monuments and church fittings of the Tudor period, and when it did eventually affect the buildings themselves, coming indirectly through France and the Low Countries.

Before turning to early Renaissance architecture in England it is helpful to look at its ultimate source — the Renaissance architecture of Italy. In the fifteenth and sixteenth centuries Italian architects took up the elements and principles of Roman architecture and made out of them a new synthesis, a learned Classical style that sought to re-create the antique mode in terms of their own time. Much was based on Vitruvius, the Roman authority on architecture, whose ideas were revived early in the fifteenth century and developed by Alberti and in the sixteenth century by Vignola and Palladio.

A distinctive feature of their approach was the way they sought a theoretical basis for architecture in mathematics and philosophy, examples of which are their theories of proportion based on mathematical ratios. In their search for harmony in plan and elevation they subjected not only the building as a whole to this intellectual discipline, but also every part of it, so that each moulding had its proper position, contour and proportion; each wall, column, pilaster, pier, arch and lintel its exact dimensions and place. The result was a highly self-conscious style, and Brunelleschi, Alberti, Bramante, Michelangelo and Palladio all show this awareness of an intellectual side to their art.

Early Renaissance building in England took place during the second half of the sixteenth century and the first quarter of the seventeenth. There was the usual time-lag between what took place in Italy and the repercussions north of the Alps. The English, however, did not follow Classical precedent with the strictness of the Italians. They did not, for example, observe the correct proportions of the orders nor did they keep the style pure, so that the result in England was a hybrid of debased Classicism and traditional English late-Gothic forms expressed in a rough symmetry.

Elizabethan

Elizabethan is a composite style deriving mainly from:

(1) the continuation of late Gothic and Tudor brick or stone structures with their triangular gables and straight-headed, mullioned and transomed bay windows;

(2) the French Renaissance style of the early sixteenth century — the style of the Loire valley chateaux from which Italian Renaissance influence was felt at one remove, as in the Gate of Virtue at Caius College, Cambridge (1564), with its triumphal arch motif on the ground floor, three superimposed orders and a triangular classical pediment;

(3) decoration from the Low Countries and Germany, such as Flemish strapwork and curved Dutch gables taken from pattern books, a new medium of communication.

Owing to the poverty of the Crown there was no royal school to set a fashion and the dominant type is the individualistic country house of the new nobility. Plans, though varied, moved towards a greater unity, those of the larger houses continuing the Tudor shapes ⌐⌐ ⌐⌐⌐ ⊢——⊣ with their emphasis on symmetry. Originally the blocks were only one room thick and therefore lit from both sides.

Until the end of the sixteenth century the hall was usually parallel to the main axis and entered from a screened passage. The courtyard house declined as the need for defence diminished, but the gatehouse is often retained as a display feature.

Elevations also show a greater unity and symmetry, opened up by numerous windows, which became a basic element of the design as at Hardwick Hall (1590). Most typically they are (whether plain or bay) large, rectangular, mullioned and transomed windows: a simple and dignified type that goes back to an earlier period, though the early Renaissance usually made them larger and more uniform. The diamond or square panes are set in lead canes. The central feature of the façade is often a two- or three-storeyed porch or pavilion with perhaps a round-arched door and superimposed orders, topped by an odd assemblage of decorative motifs, which include strapwork, obelisks, pediment and Gothic coat of arms. The porch at Kirby Hall, Northants (1575), shows French inspiration, those of Cobham (1594) Flemish. Roof lines are characteristically lively and broken with their curved or triangular gables, domed pavilions or turrets and groups of tall column-like chimneys. This is so even where there are balustraded parapets of Classical origin, and there is a general contrast with the rather more sober lower part of the façade. Robert Smithson's Wollaton (1580), however, has both an elaborate skyline and rich Flemish-Classical façades and is unusually extravagant.

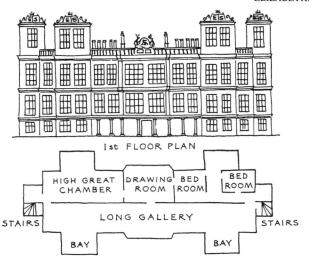

1st FLOOR PLAN

STAIRS					
	HIGH GREAT CHAMBER	DRAWING ROOM	BED ROOM	BED ROOM	
	LONG GALLERY				
BAY			BAY		STAIRS

HARDWICK HALL 1590

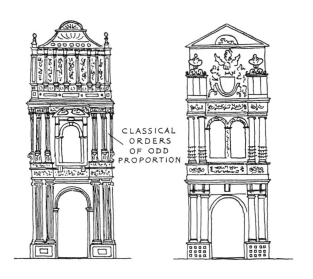

CLASSICAL ORDERS OF ODD PROPORTION

KIRBY HALL 1575   COBHAM HALL 1594

Elizabethan interiors show a tendency towards a greater number of living-rooms and shifts of emphasis in which upper-floor rooms grow in importance and the great chamber develops as the hall dwindles. A feature is the long gallery on the first floor, often running the whole length of the house, and used to display pictures and for indoor exercise, music or dancing. Walls are commonly wainscoted in oak panelling (small panels corresponding to a plank's width) or hung with tapestry. The friezes and ceilings are plastered in patterns derived from late Gothic vaults. Fireplaces have coupled columns and herms (debased caryatids) carrying elaborate overmantels embellished with geometrical patterns of strapwork, in which oval and diamond-shaped marbles and ornamental stones are set like gems. Stone staircases are still of the winding type but much broader than Gothic ones.

Ornament in general repeats the same mixture of sources already noted. Classical motifs such as mouldings, columns, small obelisks as finials and statuary rub shoulders with 'Gothic' vault designs and tangles of Flemish strapwork. Like the style itself, Elizabethan ornament is rich, fertile and vigorous at its best, at its worst coarse, dull and clumsy. But it is always strong and virile, a fit embodiment of the spirit of Elizabethan England.

Jacobean

Jacobean is the name given to the development of Elizabethan architecture in the first quarter of the seventeenth century. It is quite different from the mature Italianism of Inigo Jones, which is described in the next chapter. Compared with the earlier period a number of modifications can be observed. The great houses have a more restrained and less bizarre character, making them more Classical in feeling, but they still have enough late medieval features (such as their windows and turrets) to justify the appellation 'King Jamie's Gothic'. Hatfield House by Robert Lyminge (1607) is a good example, more typical than splendid Knole.

There is now less pretension and more comfort. Planning continues the same trends but is more compact, so that some side blocks are two rooms thick. Façades, more often now of brick, have greater areas of plain wall since windows are sometimes smaller, though still large. In late Jacobean windows many lights are replaced by four and these are sometimes crowned with a triangular or segmental pediment. Skylines are quieter. The hall now becomes specifically the entrance hall and is symmetrically placed behind the porch, often with a floor of black and white marble squares. The staircase receives special attention. Probably of sixteenth-century Spanish origin, the usual type is of oak and is in three flights arranged round an open rectangular or square well, the landing being on the fourth side. The balusters and newel

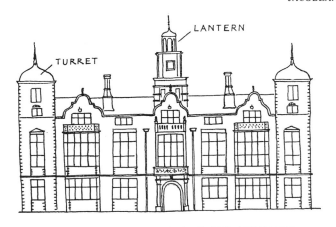

LANTERN

TURRET

BLICKLING HALL 1616 ROBT. LYMINGE

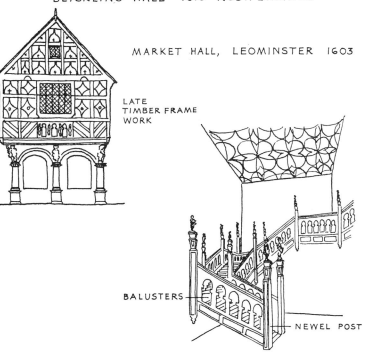

MARKET HALL, LEOMINSTER 1603

LATE
TIMBER FRAME
WORK

BALUSTERS

NEWEL POST

59

posts at the angles are enriched with Flemish-Italianate carving, including figures or heraldic beasts. Altogether it is an impressive feature, though compared with the elegance and spaciousness of later staircases its proportions are still a little cramped. Ornament is still very lavish but perhaps less fantastic.

The smaller houses of the reigns of Elizabeth I and James I continued in the Tudor manner: small stone houses in the late Gothic vernacular, or timber-framed buildings. The latter reached their peak during this period. In the early seventeenth century the frame is usually in a single piece so that overhanging storeys are discontinued, reducing the risk of fire in confined towns. The timber struts of the frame now become more widely spaced, a feature that may be the result of a greater constructional experience which was able to make more economical use of the material. On the other hand, there is much deliberate exploitation of the structural members to make elaborate patterns, and different preferences can clearly be seen by comparing the rich decoration of the north-west with that of the south-eastern counties.

There are a number of interesting colleges of this period which resemble quadrangular, late medieval country houses, with a gatehouse opposite the hall which has the master's lodging at its upper end, e.g. Trinity College, Cambridge (1604).

Finally, the formal 'Dutch' garden is another fashion from the Low Countries. The layout of walks and flower-beds bordered with box and yew hedges is geometrical, and topiary adds a touch of fantasy.

Vernacular architecture

A great many cottages and small farmhouses, though much altered through the years, survive from the period of the sixteenth to the early eighteenth century. As the poorer classes were now generally better off, their dwellings were rather more substantial than those of earlier periods, though their constructional systems were of the simplest. They have either weight-bearing walls or a timber frame. Since materials at hand were used there is a close relationship between type and region and this, together with their informal appearance and their usually low, horizontal line, keeps them in admirable harmony with their surroundings. Economy of arrangement was an important factor in their design, so that windows are small, and where there is a second storey it is often of the dormer kind since bedrooms occupy part of the roof space (another reason for this is that walls are kept deliberately low for strength on account of insufficient bonding).

Timber-frame construction, already described in the section on Tudor building, is characteristic of the north-west lowlands, the

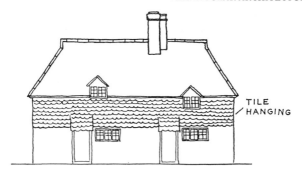

TILE
HANGING

17th CENTURY
SOUTHERN CLAY DISTRICT
COTTAGE BUILDING

west midlands and the south-east. Infilling is either wattle and daub with a coat of plaster or brick nogging, but an interesting local feature is the patterned plasterwork or pargeting of East Anglia, which covers up everything, including the timbers of the frame.

Brick is typical of clay districts such as much of the midlands. Roofs are tiled or thatched and sometimes the top half or weather gables of the buildings are tile-hung or barge-boarded with overlapping planks of elm, and in chalk districts flint, 'knapped' or squared, appears in a brick framework.

In some parts of the south-west cob (layers of pressed mud and straw coated with plaster), with rounded corners to prevent cracking, is used for walls, and roofs are thatched; but in the far west large, rough, unsquared granite stones and slates are the rule.

Stone districts possess some of the finest examples of vernacular architecture. Better-quality freestone results in a more finished appearance and there is a tradition of good carving in the historically prosperous Cotswold country. Here and elsewhere windows have stone mullions, labels or dripstones. Roof pitches are usually lower when roofing material is heavy, such as stone slabs.

Such dwellings lacked the elaboration of larger houses but the low rooms of those of the more prosperous franklins and clothiers were made handsomer and warmer by carved chimney pieces and oak panelling of the type surviving at East Riddlesden Hall, Keighley.

5. The seventeenth century

Inigo Jones

In the early part of the seventeenth century there came upon the scene a highly significant figure, Inigo Jones (1573-1652), the first English architect in the modern sense — not a master mason but one who was responsible for the entire design and its execution throughout. Beginning as a designer of scenery and costumes for court masques, Jones visited Italy twice to study the work of Palladio. As a result he brought back to England, while traditional Jacobean structures were still building, a pure Italian Renaissance style of what was then a revolutionary character. In 1615 he became Surveyor-General of Works to the Crown (i.e. chief architect), and his two seminal designs were the Queen's House at Greenwich and the Banqueting House, Whitehall.

The Queen's House (1616) is a villa based on Palladian examples, though rather longer and lower with larger windows better adapted to conditions of English light. Instead of the more ramifying early Renaissance plan it is a compact rectangle (originally two linked blocks) expressed in plain, dignified, completely symmetrical façades. The wide windows of many lights have been banished in favour of smaller, narrower and carefully proportioned rectangular windows of regular size. The broken skyline and vertical accents of gables and turrets are replaced by a strongly marked horizontal line produced by an unbroken string-course, cornice and crowning balustrade that shuts off the roof from view. This horizontality is further emphasised by the rusticated ground floor which also gives an appearance of solidity and strength. External ornament is used with extreme restraint. Almost the only features are the moulding of the cornice, the rustication and the regularly spaced Ionic columns of the first-floor central loggia.

The interior was planned in accordance with Palladian precept, with the principal rooms on the first floor or *piano nobile* (hence the loggia). The entrance hall is a mathematically harmonious cube, and the smaller rooms are in simple ratio to one another. There is ample accommodation for a staircase of a new and spacious nobility. The original interior was in deliberately rich contrast to the severity and discipline of the exterior and introduced a new note of Italianate magnificence to replace the oak wainscoting and tapestries. The best surviving Jones interior is the Double Cube Room at Wilton House (1649), one of a suite of splendid state rooms with white panelled walls. The panels are large and outlined by mouldings; the pictures are incorporated as part of the design; the ornament, chiefly palms, fruit and flowers, is in high relief and gilded. The massive overmantel and doorcase with broken pediment borne on columns are part of the room's architecture. The height of its double cube proportions is subtly modified by the coved ceiling.

BANQUETING HOUSE, WHITEHALL 1619

The Banqueting House (1619) is the only part of Jones's design for Charles I's great Palace of Whitehall that was built, but it was his most influential work. Again there is the compact rectangular plan, this time for a large hall of double cube proportions rising two storeys above a basement. The lower storey has an Ionic order, the upper a Corinthian in front of a channelled wall. Ornament and interest are derived from the alternating lower-storey window pediments, triangular and segmental, and the carved frieze of masks and swags at the level of the Corinthian capitals. The total effect resembles an Italian palace facade with details from Palladio, though it lacks his Mannerist tension and is closer in feeling to the earlier High Renaissance calm and serenity of Bramante and Raphael.

Another importation of Jones was a town-planning concept without precedent in England at that time. This was the Italian idea of the square, though the layout of the ensemble of the first — Covent Garden dating from the 1630s, with its garden on one side, two sides of uniform brick houses, and the fourth side the church of St Paul flanked by two isolated houses — is possibly derived from Henri IV's scheme for Paris. It was the prototype of much that was to follow in London and in other towns over the next two hundred years, as were Jones's terrace town houses; and together their descendants are to be seen at Bath and in the Regent's Park terraces.

The basic type of Jones's town houses is built of brick with stone dressings and has a tall, plain, dignified façade with a fenestration system later copied in Georgian buildings. This has the tallest of its rectangular windows on the first floor, now the main one, and the smallest on the top floor. At Covent Garden the houses had ground-floor loggias. Lindsay House, Lincoln's Inn Fields, with its rusticated ground floor and giant order of pilasters supporting an. entablature and balustrade, is a particularly impressive specimen.

St Paul's, Covent Garden, is the earliest surviving Classical church in England, though it was rebuilt in the eighteenth century. Its portico with Tuscan columns and pediments is modelled on sixteenth-century Italian examples and is the first one with freestanding columns in northern Europe.

Though Jones's work is in a sense derivative in that it is a conscious attempt to reproduce a sixteenth-century Italian style, it comprehends principles as well as forms and is not meticulously copyist. Without breaking the conventions, Jones knew how to practise the Renaissance tradition with vitality and modify its monumentality to suit the English temperament and scene.

His influence on domestic architecture was somewhat delayed because the style of the Queen's House was too new and startling to be assimilated quickly, and most early seventeenth-century houses are late Jacobean in style, or under contemporary Dutch influence, but with more compact planning and a Classical feeling of repose and grave dignity. Their scattering of Palladian detail, however, is as much due to Jones as to a greater familiarity with Classical forms from the study of translations of such works as Serlio's.

But some architects who came after Jones were more directly influenced by him, so much so as to form a recognisable 'school'. The classic example of their work was Coleshill House (Oxon) by Sir Roger Pratt, with Jones as consultant. Typical is Peter Mills's Thorpe Hall, near Peterborough (1653), planned as a compact block in four storeys over a basement. The main feature of the façade is the fenestration system in which the even rhythm of tall rectangular windows is relieved of monotony by the introduction of triangular and segmental pediments to the second floor and the attic. Above the strongly marked cornice rises a steeply sloping pitched roof broken by dormer windows and massive chimney stacks, all finely proportioned to the mass of the house below. The entrance is not pretentious and behind it lies the hall, the staircase still being a three-flight arrangement with pierced panelling and carving (not balusters) as was usual in the mid seventeenth century.

Mid seventeenth-century and later interiors generally show the influence of Jones, their walls having plaster or wood panelling made of larger panels now that thin sheets could be joined together. Fireplaces became simpler and more architectural with a picture frame as part of the chimney piece.

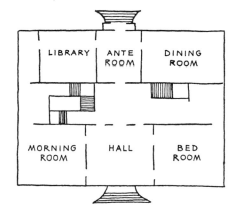

THORPE HALL 1653 P. MILLS

The style of Jones was carried forward well into the later part of the century and its influence can be seen in Trinity College Library, Cambridge, and the east end of St Paul's Cathedral, both by Wren. It also inspired the Palladians of the eighteenth century who found Baroque too extravagant for their taste and saw in Jones the purest English exponent of Renaissance architecture.

WEST FRONT

ST. PAUL'S ·CATHEDRAL 1675-1710

Christopher Wren

The second great name of the seventeenth century is that of Christopher Wren (1632-1723), a man of many parts who, in addition to being an artist, epitomised the scientific spirit of his time and did not specialise in architecture until after the Great Fire of 1666 when he was appointed Surveyor-General.

Though Wren continued the Classical trends of Jones, he also came under the influence of contemporary French work in his public buildings and Dutch in his domestic ones. Out of these he produced a version of Classicism that was original, not only because it inclined to the Baroque, but more importantly because it was an Anglicised Classicism with a distinct national character such as had not yet appeared in England. His structural skill was remarkable, as can be seen from the double dome of St Paul's, and this is marked by a masterly use of traditional materials and by the Portland stone which he introduced to London and which later became so popular.

Wren's principal work was St Paul's Cathedral (1675-1710). The design shows him embracing ideas from several sources, yet making out of them a great building which bears unmistakably the stamp of his originality.

The plan combines the central plan of the Renaissance (originating in Byzantine architecture), as exemplified in St Peter's, Rome, and the Latin cross of the middle ages. The Jones-like east end of its Italian-palace exterior façades has already been mentioned. The coupled columns of the imposing west front derive from Perrault's Louvre, and the flanking towers are Baroque. The reposeful dome is splendidly Classical but the lantern is not. The colonnade round the drum is Classical but not the variety of its alternating niches and loggias. The interior walls and piers have niches and hollows which endow them with plasticity and something of the Baroque quality of movement, and there is a complication and flow of space in the way windows are cut into vaults and saucer domes. In sum, it appears a highly individual blend of Classical and Baroque elements.

Besides St Paul's, Wren was responsible for the rebuilding of over fifty London churches destroyed by the Great Fire. These city churches were the first to be built since the middle ages and being post-Reformation were conceived as preaching halls suitable for Protestant services centred on the sermon.

Their plans reveal the intellectual basis of Wren's art by their underlying geometry. They are very varied and cleverly adapted to the small awkwardly shaped sites at his disposal, and they succeed in retaining a remarkable sense of space. Exteriors are usually plain and boxlike, full of Classical repose, but set off by one of his highly inventive and elaborate steeples, which show him trans-

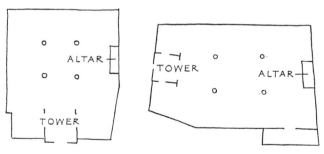

ST. MARTIN LUDGATE   ST. MARY AT HILL

lating the Gothic spire into the language of Classical forms. They are tall and many-tiered, beautifully proportioned and ingenious in both construction and variety of design.

Their interiors are large, clean rooms, well lit by big windows and decorated with white plasterwork and gold leaf. Extra accommodation is provided by a gallery. The altar is now a simple table, often placed in the body of the church. The general effect is lucid and logical and therefore Classical, but the Baroque tendencies already noted in St Paul's are also present. At St Stephen, Walbrook, the saucer dome rests on eight arches supported by

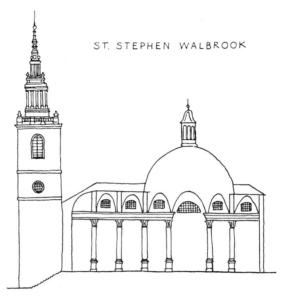

ST. STEPHEN WALBROOK

twelve slim columns, an arrangement that leads to a Baroque confluence of spaces.

Associated with the architecture of Wren is a fine school of English craftsmanship which included Tijou, maker of wrought iron grilles and staircases, Grinling Gibbons, the naturalistic wood carver, Thornhill, the painter of murals and ceilings in a Baroque style, and Cibber the sculptor.

The smaller-scale domestic architecture of the late seventeenth and early eighteenth centuries was one of the most successful solutions to the problem of how to combine comfort and moderate size with spaciousness and the dignity of a Classical design. The type is commonly known as the 'Queen Anne' house, though it is of Dutch origin, is not confined to England and was already established in the 1680s before Queen Anne came to the throne. The earliest example seems to be Eltham Lodge (1663) by Hugh May, but the type chiefly evolved here under Wren.

There are local variations but the general characteristics are as follows. Plans are simple rectangles of Classical proportions,

FENTON HOUSE, HAMPSTEAD 1693

A 'QUEEN ANNE' HOUSE

SHELL CANOPY

ARCHI-TRAVE

SEGMENTAL PEDIMENT

BULL'S EYE WINDOW

BELTON HOUSE 1689

though sometimes short wings are added. The plain brick façades are symmetrical with a pedimented centre and Classical rectangular windows with thick wooden glazing bars. Windows are of the sash type, imported from Holland in the 1680s. Doorways, of which there are many kinds, have triangular or rounded pediments or 'shell' canopies, usually supported by brackets or attached half columns. Roofs are of a steep pitch, hipped and without gables, and strongly marked off from the façade by a cornice or eaves-line. Above this there is often an attic to provide third-storey accommodation without spoiling the Classical proportions of the elevation by making it too tall. Projecting dormers, following Jones and Webb, have triangular and curved pediments. Chimneys are rather large.

The chief ornament to these houses is in the form of stone quoins and dressings. The windows are framed by architraves of 'long and short' work and have a carved keystone or scroll at their heads.

Only in the larger versions were the main rooms on the first floor. They are large, simple in plan and of dignified proportions, well-lit and comfortably panelled. Ceilings are either plain or enriched with high relief plasterwork of fruit and flower designs in the bold naturalistic style of the period. The generous three-flight staircases round an open well often have turned or spiral balusters. Fireplaces are heavy and architectural, the earlier ones sometimes pedimented.

The total result of such an arrangement of features was an uncommonly satisfying design: serviceable and functional yet aesthetically pleasing. It is no wonder that the basic type has never really gone out of favour.

Town houses of the period may be distinguished from later Georgian ones by their 'Queen Anne' treatment of doors and windows and their prominent stone dressings.

6. The eighteenth century

Baroque architecture

The work of Wren extends into the eighteenth century and it is out of his last work, Greenwich Hospital, the most grandiloquent in spirit, that the next stylistic phase in English architecture emerges. This is English Baroque, a version of a style which began in Italy in the early seventeenth century and later spread across Europe in an exuberant wave.

Baroque is a Classical Renaissance architecture that developed in a highly original and often un-Classical way, sacrificing rules and conventions in order to achieve arresting effects of grandeur and complexity, richness and movement. Typical of its features are giant double columns and pilasters, grandiose curves of volutes, scrolls and even walls, emphatic projections and recessions, broken pediments and twisted columns. Baroque is sensuous and emotional in spirit and has none of the intellectual calm of Classical art. Its exaggeration is theatrical but it is not in any sense two-dimensional, for it is at once monumental and superbly conscious of space. Its forcefulness and ostentation are contrary to English reticence, but for the short time it was practised here it produced some remarkable buildings.

Wren's pupil, Nicholas Hawksmoor (1661-1736), continued where Wren left off, designing for the growing suburbs of London churches that have the same free inventiveness and grasp of architectural values, though they seem colder and more forbidding than Wren would have made them. Their plan is original and they are massively constructed in bold heavy forms, all but one with imposing and dramatic towers in which Hawksmoor, like his master, translates an essentially Gothic motif into the Classical idiom of his day.

Sir John Vanbrugh (1664-1726), soldier and dramatist turned architect, was the pre-eminent exponent of Baroque in England. Again his work is characterised by originality, but there is an even greater leaning towards the massive and the portentous. Huge masses of masonry and cyclopean columns struggle against one another in compositions of tremendous weight and heroic grandeur. In the rich profusion of forms the Baroque spirit is everywhere. When compared with continental work, however, it is evident that Vanbrugh is still something of a Classicist, for his work is more static than dynamic and despite a certain Flemish coarseness of detail he still relies for his main effect upon broad architectural grouping and scale, rather than upon profuseness of detail and movement. For all the diversity of his exterior compositions, his plans as represented by Blenheim Palace and Castle

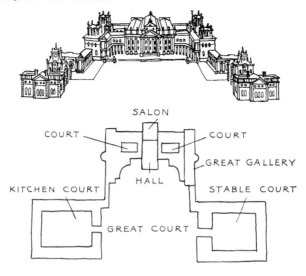

BLENHEIM PALACE 1705 J. VANBRUGH

Howard have a magnificent unity. Deriving from the Palace of Versailles or Palladio's villas with wings, they are symmetrical arrangements with a central *corps de logis* with massive outstretched wings, each one of which embraces a smaller court.

Though Vanbrugh's country houses have often been criticised as inconvenient and lacking in utility, it should be remembered that these great houses were designed primarily as ceremonial buildings and to form a suitable background against which their owners could display the art treasures which they had collected on their tours through Europe. It is by such standards that they should be judged.

Palladianism

After the first twenty years of Baroque experiment and innovation English architecture settled down in the 1730s to a more sober period of what became known as Palladianism. This was a version of Classicism in vogue for country houses (town houses were little affected), based on the villas built by Palladio in the Veneto during the sixteenth century. Inigo Jones, it will be recalled, was the first to hark back to Palladio, but the eighteenth-century fashion was much more widespread, involving a number of architects under the patronage of Lord Burlington, among whom were William Kent (1684-1778), the designer of the Horse Guards, Colen Campbell (Mereworth Castle) and Leoni (Lyme Hall). The movement was considerably influenced by the publication of a fine edition of Palladio in 1716, followed by the works of Jones in 1727. And like Palladio, the Burlington circle were guided by the precepts of Vitruvius, the Roman writer on architecture.

Lord Burlington's house at Chiswick is a transcription of the Villa Rotonda but the usual plan has a central block flanked by wings, like Prior Park by John Wood the elder (1700-54). Holkham (by Kent) and Kedleston (by Paine), however, were designed to have four angle pavilions connected to their *corps de logis*. All have the immensely dignified pedimented portico to give an imposing central accent to the composition.

Compared with their originals, English Palladian villas are larger and more solid and there is greater variety in room shapes and details. On the whole the style did not produce masterpieces in England. It is aloof, conventional and at its worst even dull. But after the excesses of Baroque its restraint and lack of bombast

PAVILION   PORTICO

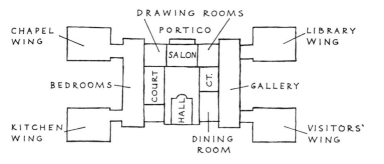

HOLKHAM   HOUSE   1734   W. KENT

were more in keeping with eighteenth-century taste and temper. Certainly its insistence on canons had a most salutary effect on the ordinary Georgian building tradition, since it firmly established 'rules of proportion' and standards of decency and taste that percolated down to the jobbing builder.

The best rooms of some of the smaller houses of the period were panelled in pine, now preferred to oak, though both were painted; but the great houses had their plaster walls decorated with architectural details and mouldings that incorporated the paintings and stucco reliefs as integral parts of the total scheme. Some of the state rooms still have walls lined with silk or velvet damask and ceilings that are elaborately patterned, painted and gilded. The new Chinese wallpaper came into use, and Roman statuary was much in evidence both inside and out.

In the early years of the century the formal, symmetrical garden layout based on Le Notre's work at Versailles, with its canals, basins, alleys and radiating walks, was preferred. But the work of London and Wise in this style was soon to give way to a new conception. Parallel with the evolution of the Palladian country house there developed the art of landscape gardening, initiated by Kent and reaching a peak in the designs of Lancelot 'Capability' Brown (1715-83). Prior Park illustrates the mid eighteenth-century ideal. Sited on a gentle slope, its spreading wings relate it to a large landscaped park, a formal house in an informal park or 'English garden', which became a European taste. The park, however, was anything but natural. Sweeping lawns, gentle hills, groves and serpentine lakes were all very carefully contrived at great labour and expense and furnished with a romantic sprinkling of temples, mausoleums, Classical bridges and the like. The aim was a picturesque composition in a piquant, artificial manner which appealed to the sophisticated taste of the *cognoscenti,* formed by contemplating the fashionable landscapes of Claude and Poussin, painters of heroic or idyllic Classical scenes set mainly in the Roman Campagna. The material means and power of the landed magnates who commissioned these houses and parks was so great that if an ancient and untidy village impaired the view it was demolished and rehoused elsewhere, as at Milton Abbas, Dorset, and Harewood, West Yorkshire.

Later Georgian architecture

In the second half of the eighteenth century the Palladian tradition continued but became less homogeneous. Sir William Chambers (1726-96) built in a more eclectic style that incorporated contemporary French influences. He adapted Palladianism to the needs of a public building housing the expanding bureaucracy of the day. In Somerset House he produced for the Admiralty and

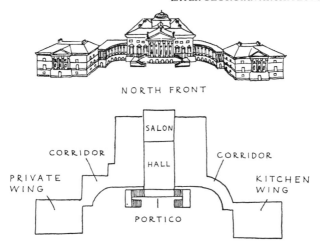

NORTH FRONT

KEDLESTON HALL 1761

BUILT BY R. ADAM FROM A DESIGN BY J. PAINE
ORIGINALLY TO HAVE HAD TWO MORE PAVILIONS

Departments of State a design remarkable for its polish and refined Classicism, though one that remains perhaps too domestic in scale and lacking in the necessary grandeur.

The outstanding name from the 1760s onwards is that of Robert Adam (1728-92), the most famous of the Adam brothers. After studying Roman architecture and publishing his drawings of Diocletian's Palace at Spalato he set to work designing country houses. His exteriors are modified Palladianism and his bent may be judged by comparing earlier Palladian work with the slender grace of the portico at Osterley and the echoing curves and lighter touch of the south front at Kedleston.

But Adam made himself responsible for the entire scheme and his most original work was done on the interiors. There he and his team of artists created a new style of decoration, based upon his imaginative reinterpretation of chiefly Roman motifs, in an attenuated and lively style executed with great delicacy and refinement. The heavy stiffness and pomposity of much Palladianism is replaced by a new and subtle chasteness. The Roman plaster technique of hard stucco which Adam revived was admirably suited as a medium for his richly varied though always crisp and elegant ornament. Especially characteristic are his ceilings, sometimes delicately tinted, with their shallow curved mouldings and painted panels and medallions. Although he has been called 'the father of the Classical Revival' on account of his interest in original Roman sources, there is little of Roman *gravitas* in his work and his rhythms are closer to Rococo. Though occasionally he is a little saccharine for some tastes, at his best he is quite incomparable.

Adam's country house plans are usually complex, appropriate to the aristocratic life they served. Original features are their un-Palladian employment of curves and effects of spatial movement. Both are exemplified in his use of alcoves and apses, especially when screened by columns with an entablature open above the cornice, and in his interior domes and wall niches.

ADAM'S USE OF ALCOVE, APSE
& OPEN SCREEN OF COLUMNS

His town houses are conventional eighteenth-century houses except for the original interiors. He was, however, the first major architect to apply a 'palace façade' to a London terrace.

Other features popularly associated with the Adam style are doorways with webbed fanlights, tall well-proportioned windows with narrow glazing bars, and elegant white marble fireplaces, all of which belong to most late Georgian buildings. His influence did, however, affect a great deal of the art-work produced in the last thirty years of the century, including Sheraton furniture,

Wedgwood pottery and silverware. Abroad it made an eventual contribution to the Empire Style.

One of the elements of eighteenth-century culture was the undercurrent of Romanticism that flowed with increasing strength beneath the broad expanse of Classicism and reason. One aspect of this was an incipient medieval Revivalism which was to become a main preoccupation of the next century.

Gothic never quite died out in England, and the vernacular farmhouses of stone districts like the Cotswolds and the Pennines are clearly based on the later manifestations of this style. Perpendicular work was done at Oxford in the seventeenth century and there is Hawksmoor's quadrangle at All Souls in the early eighteenth. But generally at this time it was commonly regarded as a barbaric style, as its name suggests, and there were few who, like Vanbrugh, felt its picturesque and associational appeal. Though he built Blackheath and gave a suggestion of the medieval castle to the sombre massing of Blenheim and Seaton Delaval, it was not until the late eighteenth century that fashionable taste followed him and found expression in the romantic and picturesque 'Gothick' fancy of Walpole's Strawberry Hill and Wyatt's Fonthill. Complete with matching interiors of delicate plaster fan vaulting, such dilettante medievalism had little in common with the seriousness of the Victorian Gothic Revival.

Another offshoot of the Rococo spirit was the fashion for *chinoiserie* that produced such oddities as Chambers's pagoda at Kew, Chippendale's Chinese-style furniture and, eventually, by an extension of this orientalism, the pavilion at Brighton early in the next century. This and the taste for porcelain afford a neat example of the interaction of economics and aesthetics, since both were made possible by the expansion of overseas trade and in their turn stimulated the import of tea, china, silk and wallpapers.

By the late seventeenth century the well-to-do in London were already living in a standardised type of terrace house that was to remain fundamentally unchanged throughout the following century. The English have generally preferred to live in the country rather than in the town when they could afford to do so, and town houses were often regarded only as *pieds-a-terre* by people who considered their main home a country house in the Shires. Hence they remained modest and unpretentious for the most part, unlike the 'hotels' of the French aristocracy in Paris.

Construction is in either brick or stone on a simple rectangular plan. The street frontage is relatively narrow but runs up to four storeys. Dividing walls are thick to reduce the fire risk and accommodate the flues. The entrance is placed to one side, approached by steps, and leads forward to the staircase. Front doors are large and panelled with semicircular fanlights to give light to the hall and are usually pedimented or topped with a semicircular arch and often flanked by Classical columns.

Opening off the hall are a large front room and a large back room, with two similar rooms on each floor. The principal feature of the façade is the fenestration scheme which reaches back to Italian Renaissance prototypes. Carefully proportioned for visual effect, windows are usually shorter on the ground floor to give an impression of solidity, taller on the first floor for importance, shorter again above and finally, to check the upward movement of the eye, very short on the top floor. The result is most dignified. Windows are of the sash type with thin wooden glazing bars, and the repeated pattern of regular-sized panes acts as a unifying feature, relating not only the separate windows of a single house front, but also façade to façade, since all conform to the same proportions. This is one of the reasons for the harmonious effect which we usually associate with a street of Georgian houses.

By the late eighteenth century it was frequently the practice to conceal the sloping slate roof of lower pitch by means of a parapet above the cornice, and chimneys were made less prominent. The general tendency as the century aged was towards greater simplicity and refinement, pointing forward to the elegance of the early nineteenth-century Regency spas.

Houses like these, arranged in terraces, formed building units that were both economical and graceful, and in many ways their replacement by sprawling suburban villas is a matter for regret.

It was Inigo Jones, first in the field in so many ways, who took the step from straight street to square in his Covent Garden, based on an Italian piazza, built about 1630. It was not, however, until the later seventeenth century that the square became popular, though once established it became one of London's most characteristic features and a great many were built between 1720 and 1860. Their dignified grace and urbanity may be regarded as a fine English achievement in the art of town planning. Though each was a self-contained compartment, the surrounding houses were not monotonously identical and there was scope for attractive variations within the accepted conventions.

Just as the English love of nature found expression in the juxtaposition of Palladian country house and landscaped park, so it did in the central garden introduced into the town square. It was a picturesque feature contrasting pleasantly with the formality of the architecture.

Later practitioners continued the square but leavened its use with new shapes such as the circus, crescent, oval and polygon; one led into the other, opening them up and breaking down their former separateness.

Another later innovation was John Wood's use of the 'palace façade' to impose unity on the terrace. In Queen Square, Bath, he gave the terrace a central portico with pediment and corner blocks, linking them with a giant order in the Palladian manner.

John Wood the Younger combined both these contemporary tendencies in the Royal Crescent, Bath, where he designed a terrace in which a giant Ionic order binds together some thirty houses into a semi-elliptical palace façade, which looks down on to an open, gently sloping sweep of turf that heightens the resemblance to a Palladian mansion.

As already noted, Adam introduced the palace frontage to London in the Adelphi terrace (now destroyed), and the motif appears again in John Nash's Regent's Park terraces of the early nineteenth century.

Not all eighteenth-century architects fit neatly into stylistic categories of the period. James Gibbs, for example, inclined to the Baroque in his powerful Radcliffe Library at Oxford but to a more restrained Palladianism in his Senate House, Cambridge.

Besides the Woods, the work of other regional designers such as Carr of York, Smith of Warwick, Harrison of Chester, and the Bastards of Dorset did much to enhance the Georgian scene.

No summary of town buildings of the eighteenth century would be complete without some reference to Georgian public building. The town halls, assemblies and customs houses had all the virtues of the ordinary domestic architecture. They are full of 'good sense': neat, well-proportioned, serviceable and in perfect harmony with one another. The shops in particular with their curved or flat patterned window fronts and elegantly lettered fascias are in agreeable contrast to the strident commercial assertiveness of some shop fronts today. No century before or since could integrate a street of diverse buildings in a more graceful and well-mannered way than the eighteenth century.

1767

ROYAL CRESCENT, BATH   J. WOOD THE YOUNGER
A PALACE FRONT IMPOSED ON TERRACE HOUSES

7. The nineteenth century

Regency architecture

The Regency style of the first thirty years of the nineteenth century represents the last phase of Georgian Classicism, simplified and modified by Adam's influence in the direction of further elegance and refinement. Some consider it to have been at the cost of robustness — it is certainly lighter and gayer.

Its typical buildings are domestic: the brick-built terraces of Brighton, Cheltenham and Leamington, faced with painted stucco, an inexpensive material for achieving the effect of a smooth stone surface and of carved stone ornamental details. Windows are tall and narrow with very thin glazing bars and their surrounds are plain and clean-cut, a design that enhances the simplicity of the façades. Curved bays and garden windows were fashionable features of the time, together with elegant wrought-iron veranda balconies, some with convex 'Chinese' roofs. Doorways are often round-headed. Roofs are low-pitched with Italianate projecting eaves. Some are flat. Decoration is sparingly applied, invariably Classical, and favours 'Grecian' motifs and Ionic or Doric columns rather than Corinthian.

The dominant figure in Regency architecture was John Nash (1752-1835), whose symmetrical terraces at Regent's Park (1811-25) with their pediments, side pavilions and giant stucco columns continue the unified eighteenth-century palace-façade treatment. He could also build in various exotic styles as required: the Indian of Brighton Pavilion, Gothic or Italianate country houses, and *cottages ornés* — for the taste for Revivalism was already established.

Nash's talent also embraced the art of town planning. It was he who conceived the organic scheme for London's West End, linking Regent's and St James's Parks with Regent Street (since rebuilt in feeble Classic), relating it to Buckingham Palace and Whitehall, and creating round Regent's Park a new upper-class residential district of noble terrace houses and picturesque landscaped park. That he was able to do all this without the autocratic powers of a Napoleon is a tribute to his resourcefulness.

Sir John Soane (1753-1837) was a contemporary of Nash but very different and highly original. Reacting from the more popular Adam, he evolved a personal style that blended highly imaginative interiors with a Grecian severity of detail. His works are few, but his austerity, crisp line, simplicity of surface and feeling for cubic relations and space are all to be seen at his own house in Lincoln's Inn Fields, now the Soane Museum (1812). These are characteristics which anticipate something of the twentieth century despite the elements of the antique.

25. Audley End, Essex: a many-windowed, turreted Jacobean palace; Perpendicular-Tudor in tradition influenced by early Renaissance symmetry and given porches with superimposed orders.

26. Wollaton Hall, Nottingham: Robert Smythson's exuberant imagination has produced a unique essay in the Italian Renaissance style modified by Flemish detail.

27. *The Queen's House, Greenwich: the restrained, scholarly, Italianate Classicism of Inigo Jones's facade was something of an architectural revelation in the reign of Charles I.*

28. *The Double Cube Room, Wilton House, Wiltshire: Palladian proportions are a feature of this splendid white and gold state apartment into which the Van Dycks are architecturally placed.*

29. St John's College, Oxford: a classically arcaded cloister and centrepiece with coupled orders and segmental pediment grafted on to an essentially Tudor building.

30. *Clare College, Cambridge: the early Stuart rebuilding by John Westley, master mason, shows the persistence of Tudor-Gothic in college vernacular, despite Classical touches.*

31. *The Sheldonian Theatre, Oxford: Wren's first building, based on Roman precedent. The wide-spanning trussed roof is characteristic of his technical inventiveness.*

32. Trinity College Library, Cambridge: something of Roman gravitas. The arches are ingeniously blocked in to allow the low floor level without impairing correct Classical proportions.
33. Dyrham Park, Avon, by William Talman, architect of Chatsworth. The modelling of the detail is typical of the period. Early sash windows and panelled interiors.

34. Castle Howard, North Yorkshire: the grand scale of English Baroque. Vanbrugh's masterpiece for the Earl of Carlisle, a potent symbol of Whig political power and high taste.

35. Blenheim Palace, Woodstock, Oxfordshire: with its wide-spread but unified plan and heroic Baroque elevations this is the most dramatic and ceremonious 'house of parade'.

36. Fydell House, Boston, Lincolnshire: a town house of 1726. Brick with stone dressings. A powerfully framed facade with giant pilasters and heavy cornice and balustrade.

37. *Stowe House, Buckinghamshire: a dignified eighteenth-century Palladian composition with portico and side pavilions, set in William Kent's superbly landscaped park with lakes and temples.*

38. *Antony House, Cornwall: the finest eighteenth-century house in the county; architect unknown. It achieves elegance despite the use of granite-like elvan as a building stone.*

39. Pulteney Bridge, Bath, Avon. Robert Adam's unusual bridge, with a superstructure of shops, links the town with the new development across the Avon.

40. *Faversham Town Hall, Kent: a polite Georgian version of a type of building often found as a traditional feature of the English country town.*

41. *Fairlynch Museum, Budleigh Salterton, Devon: a charming essay in artificial rusticity — a cottage orné with Gothick windows and a roof of Devon thatch.*

42. *The Royal Pavilion, Brighton, East Sussex: the oriental picturesque. An exotic Indian style (though with individual touches) by John Nash to serve the pleasure-loving Prince Regent.*

43. *Pelham Crescent, Hastings, East Sussex: John Kay's urbane late Georgian terrace with Regency bow windows and verandas. Note the use of stucco finish and ironwork.*

44. The Ashmolean Museum, Oxford: the Greek Revival of C. R. Cockerell's Ionic portico is a design with the liberal humanist associations suited to the building's purpose.

45. Knebworth House, Hertfordshire: the romantic novelist Bulwer-Lytton's nostalgic literary conception of Tudor as the English 'national style', on an original core.

46. *The Law Courts, London: Victorian Gothic Revival. The grouping of its features by G. E. Street is admirably adapted to the restricted views obtainable of so large a building in town.*

47. *Mentmore, Buckinghamshire: designed by Joseph Paxton and his son-in-law. Mediocre pastiche for a moneyed client. The central great hall is top-lit from a glass roof.*

48. *Saltash, Cornwall: the architecture of engineering. I. K. Brunel's Victorian railway masterpiece strikingly compares with the modern suspension bridge over the river Tamar.*

49. *The Houses of Parliament, London, 1837-60; a national symbol resulting from an architectural competition won by Charles Barry and A.W.N. Pugin.*

50. *The Palm House, Kew, 1844-8; pioneering composite use of glass and iron designed by Decimus Burton and Richard Turner.*

PRINCE'S STREET, LOTHBURY
A REGENCY FACADE 1808 J. SOANE

Revivalism

The underlying theme of nineteenth-century architecture is, however, Revivalism. Classical revival of the antique, as distinct from Renaissance architecture, began in the second half of the eighteenth century with the publication of archaeological research like Revett's *Antiquities of Athens* (1762) in which Greek and not Roman Doric appeared for the first time and shocked the Palladians and Adam. There were others though, 'Athenian' Stuart among them, who paved the way for purist Neo-Greek (1820-40), a scholarly, academic style expressive of the ideals of contemporary culture and quite suited to large public buildings such as Robert Smirke's British Museum (1823). It is not, however, merely imitative, for behind the British Museum's Ionic front the grouping of the composition is Palladian still, and the triumphal arch, now demolished, at the entrance to Euston Station was a Roman motif, not Greek. Successful essays in this manner are Charles Cockerell's provincial branches of the Bank of England.

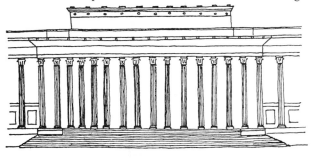

ST. GEORGE'S HALL, LIVERPOOL 1839
H. L. ELMES, COMPLETED BY C. R. COCKERELL

97

By the mid century Neo-Greek had been ousted on the Classical side by a Neo-Renaissance style chiefly inspired by the High Renaissance architecture of Rome. Early examples are Sir Charles Barry's Travellers' Club (1829) and Reform Club (1837). The style is at once richer and more materialistic, in keeping with the commercial prosperity of Victorian England. And though the Classical Revival reached its peak in the 1860s, the Graeco-Roman tradition staggered wearily on into the first decades of the twentieth century.

Gothic Revival also began in the late eighteenth century, this time as the rather frivolous and fanciful 'Gothick'. But with the more serious cult of the middle ages which was part of early nineteenth-century Romanticism, it became a very different thing.

A. W. N. Pugin (1812-52), the first serious exponent of Gothic Revival, was a medieval enthusiast, architect and writer who not only admired the aesthetic and religious values of the middle ages but saw in their structural principles and logical ornament the true essence of architecture. This was at a time when structure was of less interest to the average architect than a Classical façade, to which had been applied a great deal of heavy and often rather coarse, obscuring decoration. Pugin himself, however, had a genuine flair for decorative design, so that he was able to give to Barry's basically Classical plan and Palladian river front of the new Houses of Parliament (1836) a national colouring of Perpendicular detail that is amplified by the aspiring medieval verticality and romantic asymmetry of the towers and spires.

But generally Pugin and the later Gothicists preferred Early English: 'morally' it was a purer style. Some were more eclectic or went abroad for inspiration. At its worst much of their work is crude and inappropriate, but a few architects, out of a deep understanding of the real nature of Gothic, did succeed in creating buildings that were in effect contemporary reinterpretations of the style. Archaeological knowledge and refinement belong most to the last quarter of the century (e.g. J. L. Pearson's Truro Cathedral, 1880). The best-known Gothicist is perhaps Sir Gilbert Scott (St Pancras Hotel, 1866), but the most original was William Butterfield, whose Keble College Chapel, Oxford (1870), though using only the common bricks, timbers and tiles of the ordinary builder, genuinely recreates Gothic without affected antiquarianism and displays a remarkable individuality in its odd proportions, dramatic outline and textural ornament.

In the 'battle of the styles' both the main traditions had their supporters, but by the end of the century it was tacitly consented that Gothic Revival was suitable for ecclesiastical and scholastic buildings, and a ponderous Neo-Classical for civic buildings and business premises, while designers of country houses (like Anthony

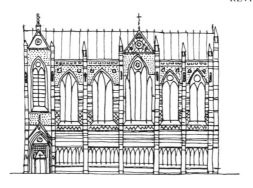

KEBLE COLLEGE CHAPEL, OXFORD 1867
WM. BUTTERFIELD

Salvin) reproduced medieval castles and Tudor, Elizabethan and Jacobean great houses. It was chiefly a question of association, since the central aristocratic tradition of the eighteenth century had come to an end in the confusion of Victorian middle-class historical Romanticism, which was more concerned with picturesqueness than with aesthetics or functional expression.

The most successful buildings of the age were its public buildings, such as town halls, market halls and exchanges. Many of them — public libraries, museums, art galleries, infirmaries, banks, offices, mechanics' institutes, workhouses and prisons — were virtually new types. Money was not spared on their elaborate façades and, though many had new and flexible plans, this

A 'GOTHIC' TOWN HALL

fundamental aspect was unfortunately by no means a preoccupation of their architects. Outside London the most typical
products survive in the industrial midlands and particularly in the
towns and cities of the north.

Engineering architecture

While the architect *per se* was studiously busy with styles and
traditional materials, casting his mind nostalgically backwards to
a romanticised past, the engineer, that representative of a new
profession born of nineteenth-century industrial technology, was
experimenting with structures like the great suspension bridges:
Menai (1819) by Thomas Telford and Clifton (1831) by I. K.
Brunel. They welcomed the challenge of the problem posed by the
needs of a new kind of society and new materials.

Cast-iron was used from the beginning of the century and steel
after 1855. Cast-iron stanchions combined with traditional load-
carrying walls produced some impressive utilitarian industrial
buildings. Telford's St Katharine's Dock warehouses (1824) and
some of the early Pennine and Cotswold textile mills are impressive not only on account of their massive bulk, but because of
the dignified simplicity deriving from their sense of scale and
proportion, and functional integrity. Though the engineer need
not necessarily possess the sensibility of the architect, it so hap-
pened that the greatest nineteenth-century engineers were
naturally gifted with a sense of form and designed structures
which were not only practical and efficient but also aesthetically
satisfying.

Iron and steel also made possible wide-spanning roof trusses
carrying an envelope of glass. This and the new tendency for
traditional craftsmanship to give way to factory production of
standard parts are both illustrated by Joseph Paxton's Crystal
Palace. Its structural system was independent of weight-bearing
walls and roofed over a vast space without internal supports, while
its cast-iron girders and glass sheets were all prefabricated and
assembled on the site. Techniques like these bore fruit in the great
railway termini with their characteristic 'barrel vaults' of glass
stretching over great volumes of space, supported by an intricate
lattice-work structure of iron members in tension (e.g. I. K.
Brunel's roof of Paddington Station, 1854). The boatstore at the
Royal Naval Dockyard, Sheerness (1858-60), is an iron-framed
structure whose elevations foreshadow the twentieth century.

Domestic architecture

Before turning to domestic architecture, mention must be made
of the proselytising work of John Ruskin and his disciple William
Morris. The former was a protagonist of Gothic whose precepts

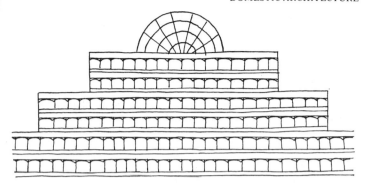

CRYSTAL PALACE, GREAT EXHIBITION 1851
J. PAXTON

often led to absurd imitations of the Doge's Palace, but who indirectly did useful work in drawing attention to the sociological and functional aspects of architecture and in reconsidering the whole question of structure, materials and workmanship. Morris attempted to apply Ruskin's theories and his insistence on the basic importance of good design had a salutary effect on the decorative arts. But he failed to come to terms with the new technology as Gropius did later at the Bauhaus.

It was for Morris that Philip Webb built the Red House, Bexleyheath (1859), which is a landmark in domestic building, the forerunner of the 'garden city' house. It has the sturdiness of late

THE RED HOUSE 1859   P. WEBB

Gothic, pointed arches and a medieval picturesqueness; but its plain red-brick walls, steep roofs and segment-headed sash windows derive from Queen Anne and the vernacular cottage architecture of the south-east. The craftsmanly feeling for traditional materials is typical of Webb. Though the immediate results of the Red House were not spectacular, its influence on succeeding villa architecture was considerable.

The eighteenth-century concept of the villa was a modest country house, secluded and informal, the merchant's retreat. By about 1800 it had moved nearer the town, and in small estates of detached houses it offered an alternative to the terrace town house. Influenced by the prevailing architectural fashions, its style changed every twenty years or so through the century: Greek, Italian, Gothic, Queen Anne and Tudor. Finally in the 1930s came the pseudo-modern villa with flat roof and corner windows, though the basic design altered little. The typical larger Victorian villa had many rooms making its plan complex and crowded, and its silhouette was often broken and picturesque.

Each house had, extravagantly, its own garden to secure a semi-rural privacy. The semi-detached villa was a cheaper compromise which used less land and became the standard middle-class dwelling. One feature was the improved plumbing. The WC was known in Queen Elizabeth I's time but was not found in the houses of the well-to-do until the last years of the eighteenth century. By the nineteenth it was a middle-class amenity, together with lavatory basins and baths by the end of the century. The working classes had to wait until the twentieth century before they could enjoy what formerly the aristocracy had to do without, though many are still waiting for a bath.

The disgrace of the age was the slum. At first the new industrial labouring classes were herded into jerry-built terraces of ugly ill-drained, insanitary boxes, back to back or round squalid dark, airless courts. Architects were not interested in social architecture and its problems, and housing provision was left to the speculative landlord and jerry-builder, checked only by the few scanty regulations of a *laissez-faire* economy. Thousands were below this level and 'cellar dwellings' without windows were commonly shared by several families. Both the Prince Consort and Lord Shaftesbury concerned themselves with the private improvement of the artisan's dwelling, and there were the early flats put up by the Peabody Trust, but there was little change until after Disraeli's housing and health acts of 1875, which empowered local authorities to enforce building regulations ensuring safe construction and sanitation and to begin slum clearance and, eventually, municipal planning and housing. After this legislation poorer houses were better built and more commodious, and the 'by-law' street of minimum width allowed more air to circulate. But there was still much drabness and ugly uniformity which showed too little regard for the quality of human environment. Some enlightened employers, however, built factory estates, such as Sir Titus Salt's Saltaire (1853) with mill, church, chapel, streets of terrace houses and a park. Later came Lever Brothers' Port Sunlight (1888) and Cadbury's Bournville (1895), planned as 'garden suburbs' in a freer, more picturesque style.

The garden city was an attempt to provide new residential communities for the growing number of people with middle-class means but discerning taste and whose ideal at that time was a suburban villa and whose progressive aesthetic was that of the arts and crafts movement, made viable by the development of modern transport facilities. The architect again re-entered the field of town planning, and before long estates of small houses in a traditional style with gables and small windows, each set in its own tree-shaded garden, began to appear outside the built-over area of towns. They differed from earlier Victorian suburbs, not only in their architectural style but also in the fact that they were designed as a whole and not piecemeal. The first was Bedford Park, Chiswick (1876), with 'Queen Anne' houses by Norman Shaw, but the full flowering did not come until the early years of the twentieth century with Letchworth, Hampstead and Welwyn. These were the prototypes of the between-wars suburb.

Norman Shaw (1831-1912) was one of the most representative and influential architects of the later nineteenth century. He was until 1870 a Gothicist, after which followed twenty years of offices, flats and country houses in a picturesque, eclectic style that owed much to Tudor half-timber, Dutch Renaissance, Queen Anne and vernacular work of the seventeenth and eighteenth centuries. His final phase was Edwardian Imperial, the somewhat pretentious decadence of Victorian Classicism. At his best Shaw is lighter and more animated than this suggests and New Scotland Yard is a happier example of his work in brick and stone.

In retrospect it becomes clear that at the close of the century certain isolated figures were at work clearing away the rank growth of imitative period styles preparatory to the cultivation of a new and more genuine one. This is evident from the greater directness and simplicity of the work of C. R. Mackintosh in the Glasgow Art School (1898), with its singular *art nouveau* interior, and also from C. F. A. Voysey's domestic designs.

Vernacular buildings lost most of their regional character in the nineteenth century, partly as a result of the uniformity of Victorian culture and partly owing to the general decline in the practice of using local materials, in the face of competition from inexpensive brick brought from outside by cheap rail transport.

8. The twentieth century
Written for this edition by Tim Buxbaum

The Grand Manner

In the early 1900s revived Gothic was a popular style for new schools and churches whilst street architecture and institutions re-animated Classicism, usually in a rather tired, derivative way; civic architecture was reassuringly solid, even ponderous, yet of high craftsmanship and rich, even extravagant, in materials such as dressed masonry, marble, polished mahogany, bevelled glass and bronze. At least three architectural voices could be heard in the pre-war years: High Edwardian Baroque reminiscent of Wren, Vanbrugh and Hawksmoor; a more up-to-date French Classicism; and a less derivative, freer approach which tried to reconcile traditional forms with advances in structural engineering.

High points of the Baroque style, with its imposing galleries and domes, are the flamboyant Central Criminal Courts of the Old Bailey, Holborn, and the War Office, Whitehall (1906, Edward Mountford), and Lancaster Town Hall (1909, William Young). More eclectic are the Victoria and Albert Museum, Kensington (1901, Sir Aston Webb), with its complex interiors and dynamic skyline, and the Prudential Assurance Buildings, Holborn (1906, Alfred Waterhouse), showing spires, gables and the exact hardness of pre-fabricated terracotta. Still Baroque in form, but logically laid out along an axis, is Cardiff City Hall and Law Courts (1897-1906), by H. V. Lanchester and Edwin Rickard.

The Anglo-French practice of Mewès and Davis (1878-1951) brought French style to the Ritz, Piccadilly (1906), hiding a sumptuous winter garden, a columned restaurant and Louis XVI interiors behind a nineteenth-century mansard-roofed Parisian façade supported on a steel frame, drawing on eighteenth-century palaces in the Place de La Concorde, Paris, and to the witty RAC Club, Pall Mall (1911), where portico sculptures include a cherub in a motor car.

French sophistication is expressed in Portland stone overlooking the Thames at County Hall, London (1908-22), by Ralph Knott, and in the buildings around Piccadilly Circus (1913-30) by Sir Reginald Blomfield. At its most refined and severe, the style became Neo-classical, a perfect language for buildings of such monumental importance as the new public façade of Buckingham Palace and the layout of the Mall (1913, Sir Aston Webb) and the even more austere King Edward VII Galleries to the British Museum (1904-14, Sir John Burnet).

Many similar buildings comprised fire-resistant floors with thin masonry walls, all supported on a steel frame, allowing long spans and fast construction. In many cases only one frontage was embellished in stone, the others remaining as utilitarian brick. In England frames were at first concealed, unlike contemporary buildings in Europe or the USA, where architects sought to demonstrate the link between the nature of their buildings and the materials from which they were composed. The most successful results of English stylistic compromise with the new structural system showed façades in masonry so pared down as to leave no doubt that they alone could never have supported the weight of any building: hence the Royal Insurance Building (1908, John Belcher) and Kodak House, Kingsway (1910, Sir John Burnet).

The Arts and Crafts Movement

Whilst civic architecture was struggling with the new vocabulary of the steel frame, a number of architects looked elsewhere seeking a practical vocabulary of design which eschewed both 'style' and self-conscious revivalism; they were not drawn to designing façades to front new steel frames. They were only marginally involved in public-sector housing. Instead they concentrated on private houses, to which they brought the forms and materials of vernacular cottages and farms, offering an easy unaffected spirit of naturalness and simplicity. Typical features are roughcast, rendered walls supporting steeply pitched overhanging roofs with tall, tapering chimneys. The resulting buildings seem born to their sites, loving the ground on which they stand: designs reflect a sense of place generated from bold composition, textural materials, delight in detail and individual character.

One of the most prolific architects of the period was C. F. A. Voysey (1857-1941), who produced forty houses for affluent middle-class clients in the period 1889-1910. Likeminded contemporaries included W. R. Lethaby, Harrison Townsend, H. M. Baillie-Scott, Leonard Stokes and Charles Rennie Mackintosh, whose Glasgow School of Art (1896-1908) combined a rich mix of Scottish vernacular, early functionalism and the sinuous elliptical curves and lovely ironwork of Art Nouveau: it was the only British building of those years to be admired abroad, especially in Vienna. Mackintosh's own house designs are best represented in Hill House, a more Baronial composition which followed in 1902-3.

The Arts and Crafts Movement produced public buildings characterised by full, rounded features and decorative craftsmanship as at Whitechapel Art Gallery and the Horniman Museum, London (1901, C. Harrison Townsend). The former never got the great Walter Crane mosaic panel intended for it. A similar fate befell Westminster Cathedral, 1903, by John Francis Bentley. It is a great asymmetric Italo-Byzantine mass of horizontally banded red brick and white stone which soars into a campanile; the powerful dark interior is sculpted into three broad shallow brick domes which were intended to be covered with mosaics.

THE ARTS AND CRAFTS MOVEMENT

Liverpool Cathedral by Giles Gilbert Scott was finally completed in 1980. It is a monumental enterprise in red sandstone, heavily buttressed, with double transepts, marking a climax of the Gothic revival, the decorative detail owing much to the Arts and Crafts Movement. The greatest religious building of the movement was All Saints, Brockhampton, Herefordshire, by William Lethaby, which brought together a thatched roof over a startling internal concrete vault in a *tour de force* of innovative shapes, architectural drama and outstanding craftsmanship.

Sir Edwin Lutyens (1869-1944) dominated English architecture for much of the first forty years of the century. His early houses, many with integral landscaping by Gertrude Jekyll, such as Deanery Garden, Sonning, Berkshire (1897), have all the material richness and variety of the best of the Arts and Crafts houses. Soft materials such as mellow stone and rubble, hand-made brick and chalk are disciplined by banded tile courses, galleting and featured patterned jointing. Equally important, the massing of the compositions is always marked by taut spatial control, esoteric proportions and dramatic geometry reinforced by the positioning of such elements as archways, balconies, oak-mullioned windows, fireplaces, chimneys and staircases, so that there is interrelationship and consistency, spreading out from the house and into the garden.

Lutyens's architecture became more disciplined with his study of the Classical Orders. A range of architectural conceits was employed, such as the use of battered walls, masonry coursing diminishing in the height of the building, and manipulation of perspective. Many can be experienced at Castle Drogo, Devon (1910-30), a dignified oak and granite composition of clean strength flooded with natural light. In contrast Lutyens's dignified Cenotaph, Whitehall (1920), apparently so simple, contains no straight lines and is a highly sophisticated study in geometry. Very large buildings included Britannic House, Finsbury Circus (1927), which broke new stylistic ground in a freely classical composition of Portland stone eight storeys high, to be followed by the powerful, richly rusticated Midland Bank off Poultry in the City of London (1939).

Lutyens, with Sir Herbert Baker, was responsible for one of the world's displays of architecture, the vice-regally splendid Government Buildings at New Delhi, India (1912-30).

1918 to 1939

After the First World War many institutions resumed building in the pre-war way. Steel-framed civic architecture continued to be stone-clad but the scale became enormous and building façades increasingly were stripped of historical references and stepped or 'massed' with strongly geometric and, especially, cubic character. In confident hands there were powerful results, for example the swaggering Port of London Authority Building (1922, Sir Edwin Cooper), London Transport Headquarters (1927-9) and Senate House (1931-2, Charles Holden) and the Cunard Building, Liverpool (Willink and Thicknesse). Perhaps the most solid and imposing building of the period was Battersea Power Station (1934), by Sir Giles Gilbert Scott, with its massive brick walls and four symmetrical giant columnar tapering smoke stacks looking like the legs of an upturned table. The RIBA building (1934, Grey Wornum) presents a striking form to Portland Place, as does the cylindrical arrangement decorated with bas-reliefs of Broadcasting House (G. Val Myer) down the road. Bush House, Aldwych (Helmle, Corbett & Harrison), has Cubist qualities which were more fully developed in structurally innovative buildings of the period. A pioneer in that field was the engineer Sir Owen Williams, who made possible the Boots Factory, Beeston, Nottinghamshire (1930), which had concrete mushroom columns, cantilevered floors and storey-height glass curtain walls. They led directly to the façade of Simpsons, Piccadilly (1935, Joseph Emberton), and Peter Jones, King's Road (1936-9, William Crabtree), where the concrete frame was wrapped round with glass walls.

The most exciting new building type was the cinema, redolent of escapism and fantasy. Art Deco (named from the Exposition of Arts Decoratives in Paris in 1925) seemed made for it: a dramatic fusion of strong geometric form, steel windows, bright colours and graphic sharpness which blossomed in neo-Egyptian glory (influenced by the discovery of Tutankhamun's tomb in 1922) through the 1920s and 1930s. The style reflected the new consumer society. The Chrysler Building, New York (1928-30), was a model, but it was best interpreted in English cinemas such as the Carlton, Essex Road (1930) and the Gaumont State, Kilburn High Road (1937), both in London and both by George Coles.

In the 1930s along the Great West Road in London prospered a cooler style of curved, white factories such as Firestone and, most famous, Hoover (1932, Wallis Gilbert & Partners). The *Financial Times* of the day called it the 'ugliest building in London'. One of the most influential buildings of the period was the curved black glass block of the Daily Express Building, Fleet Street (1931, Sir Owen Williams), its interior rich in architectural metalwork.

Modernism

For the first half of the twentieth century mainstream English architecture looked backwards, carefully updating Tudor and Georgian models. After the First World War Britain needed one million dwellings and the political race to satisfy potential demand expanded the suburbs rapidly and without control. In Europe from 1917 to 1925 there was an unparalleled explosive creativity throughout the arts which fostered a bewildering multiplicity of architectural forms.

European visions of the future ranged from strange metaphysical caverns to crystalline forms, from romantic folk cottages to sleek, flat-roofed steel and glass constructions.

It was suggested that copying the superficial motifs, ornaments and details of previous cultures and applying them to new buildings was wrong and was out of touch with the modern reality, which included automobiles, flying boats, steam engines and ocean liners. Of what relevance were a previous generation's carvings? Why not use ship's handrails, metal staircases, industrial glazing and chequer-plate floors in buildings? Why not display lifts and generators in the same way that the latest Bentley showed off its riveted steel sheets and supercharger? Modernism proselytised a new optimistic spirit arising from mass production, with standardisation and prefabrication characterising what was seen as a new social order. The previous century's preoccupation with style was rejected in favour of method, organisation and technology.

The cause was cogently argued by the architects Le Corbusier and Pierre Jeanneret in France and disseminated in England; they proclaimed a crisp clean new architecture free from old traditions. Le Corbusier produced a manifesto for a new house for a new life: reinforced concrete would allow an open plan (upper floor walls could be located anywhere) and a façade where large and long windows could be introduced to bring fresh air and light to every part (helped by new central heating). Fire risks and maintenance would be reduced. Columns carried the living area clear of the damp ground; the flat roof provided a sun garden and light top rooms instead of poky attics. Geometrically strong forms rendered applied ornament unnecessary. Rob Mallet-Stevens proclaimed there was no longer any need to carve since building itself was a carving formed of planes of light and shade; out went timber windows in favour of steel frames, which better suited this aesthetic. But cubic forms and open balconies were inevitably more successful in the sunlight of the Mediterranean than in drizzly England; the style-driven ideology and its economics were clearly at odds with architects of the English Domestic Revival and the ideals of the Arts and Crafts movement.

As the impetus for Modernism in England came from foreign architects it was originally called the International Style. After their ideas came the architects, from New Zealand, Hungary, the Caucasus and, most important, Germany, from which several fled on the closure of the influential German design school, the Bauhaus, whose philosophy was to look at construction from the point of view of technique, not historical precedent, thus always creating new forms. Refugees included that great advocate of mass-production Walter Gropius and the minimalist ('less is more') Mies van der Rohe, who went on to practise in the USA. Ernö Goldfinger and Berthold Lubetkin stayed in England. The latter formed the Tecton group of architects with the structural engineer Ove Arup, initially working at London Zoo on the Gorilla House (1934) and, more significantly, the Penguin Pool (1935), with its innovative interlocking cantilevered concrete spirals which appeared to hang freely in space and caught the imagination of the public, fusing technology and style. In terms of engineering they were revolutionary (Arup went on to design such structures as Sydney Opera House). Tecton turned to housing at Highpoint 1 and 2, Hampstead, in clean, light-painted concrete blocks with cantilevered balconies and horizontal windows. This was an auspicious start for a style of architecture which was misunderstood, misapplied, underfunded and went dreadfully wrong.

Postwar housing

Expanding industry and the seemingly endless suburban speculative housing of the 1920s and 1930s risked creating huge amorphous conurbations in contrast to Le Corbusier's vision of well-appointed and fully serviced skyscrapers in lush parkland. Green Belts and New Towns were not introduced until 1944 and only in 1947 did the Town and Country Planning Act make all land subject to control under a system intended to be regularly reviewed to allow change and flexibility whilst providing policies on matters such as zoning, parking and privacy. Faced with huge housing problems, the new public authorities saw in Le Corbusier's vision an urban solution, quickly built, with efficient mass transport, clean rationalism, order and sanitation. They misunderstood the value of existing nineteenth-century terraced housing, much of which was basically sound, although neglected and without indoor sanitation. Wholesale clearance and rebuilding, termed 'Comprehensive Redevelopment', was invoked under the new Planning Acts. To complement the clearance, the 1946 British New Towns Act initiated, amongst others, the new towns of Stevenage, Harlow, Welwyn Garden City, Hatfield, Hemel Hempstead, Bracknell, Crawley and Basildon. Their objectives included zoning between homes and work, separation of traffic and pedestrians, efficient mass transport and urban parks.

The postwar scarcity of conventional raw materials combined with spare capacity in former munitions factories presented an opportunity for prefabricated building systems. Houses bought votes, and ambitious political targets simply could not be met through traditional construction. The 1951 Labour government built 200,000 houses; in 1954 the Tories built 300,000. To cope with the vast new public housing policy there was a shift in architectural practice from small private offices to large public authorities. New, previously untried construction methods were introduced and prewar standards discarded.

Le Corbusier completed the Unité d'Habitation in Marseilles in 1952, a huge concrete block of streets in the air with communal facilities. Local authorities sought to build similarly in England.

Alton Estate, Roehampton (1953-61), and Park Hill, Sheffield (1961), are examples of concrete housing blocks linked with horizontal streets or decks, bridging from block to block for over half a mile, necessitating a long walk to shops and community facilities. The vision perhaps came closest to realisation at the Barbican (1957-79), by Chamberlin, Powell and Bon. Here a 35 acre site (heavily bombed but still with 13 acres of Georgian and Victorian terraces) was cleared and used to house six thousand people in well-appointed low- and high- rise towers sculpted into identifiable silhouettes looking over a school and arts centre laid out around water features.

Elsewhere it was different. Much shorter construction times and less prestigious locations resulted in housing built down to minimal budgets. The streets in the air had no pubs or shops, the parkland did not exist, management was poor. Deck access arrangements led to alienation, loneliness, anonymity, vandalism. Untried building systems, rapidly assembled by unskilled operatives on piecework, led to dwellings with poor insulation, cold bridging, leaks, condensation, defective heating, inadequate fire barriers or acoustic separation, windswept passages. Poor management encouraged faulty lifts, litter, graffiti, infestation by rats and cockroaches. Matters came to a head at Ronan Point in 1969 when a gas explosion in a 23-storey tower block brought down an entire corner of the building, killing five people.

Thereafter high-density concrete housing schemes were lower-rise, but the deeper problems remained: the award for good housing won by Broadwater Farm might surprise those who rioted there in the 1990s. Noteworthy housing included the Foundling Estate (1968-74), by Patrick Hodgkinson, and the great stepped concrete crescent of Alexandra Road (1973-8), by Neave Brown. Local authorities remained committed to Comprehensive Redevelopment long after they should have done: it has been estimated that 65-70 per cent of GLC housing demolished in the period 1967-71 was in fair to good condition and could have been rehabilitated. It took the efforts of the press and architects such as Rod Hackney, initially at Black Road, Macclesfield, and of Hunt Thompson, to stimulate self-help co-operatives and bring in 'community architecture'. This brought back dignity to terraced housing and in due course spread to the upgrading of decaying tower blocks, providing properly secure entrances, landscaping, carpeted landings, better lighting, porters and murals, adding pitched roofs and recladding externally with new materials.

For a time new housing increasingly took on semi-vernacular forms, as small brick units with pitched roofs, little balconies, semi-private spaces and a sense of place, typically Lillington Street, Pimlico (1961-8, Darborne and Darke), and Friar's Quay Housing, Norwich (1975, Feilden & Mawson). Publication of the Essex Design Guide, which became influential throughout England, preached a kind of

neo-vernacular style, speeding the process, which took in such public buildings as Hillingdon Civic Centre (1977, Andrew Derbyshire),
where a large bureaucratic organisation was rehoused in a pitched-
roof brick building of intimate scale. The volume house builders switched
from concrete to small detached and semi-detached units with private
gardens and garages which rarely related to surroundings beyond the
winding estate roads which served them. Estates of brick and concrete tile sprang up as quickly in the hills of Wales as in the stone
villages of middle England. Planning authorities were set the complex task of bringing character to these dreadfully similar estates
through legislation without closing the door to sensitive new development, which increasingly tried to respond to regional character.
The 1967 Civic Amenities Act brought in compulsory designation of
Conservation Areas in an attempt to maintain and enhance existing
architectural quality but not to rule out further development. Yet the
worst excesses of 1960s Brutalism, the 'NIMBY' syndrome, short-
term policies and innate English conservatism have all too often
blighted more recent attempts to contribute to such areas.

A landmark in new housing for ten thousand people was at Byker,
Newcastle (1968-81, Ralph Erskine). It sheltered behind a curving
brick ribbon wall of maisonettes, rising in a jagged roof line to eight
storeys. The rear face was studded with tiny windows because it
faced north to a road; the sunny side was open, covered with boarded
balconies and profiled sheeting in bright primary colours looking
over low-rise housing, all extensively landscaped around existing
pubs, shops, offices and a church. An architects' office was set up on
the site and people were rehoused with direct reference to their
previous neighbours and kin, maintaining a social framework within
a new milieu of soft materials, variety and bright colours. Confidence began to return to public housing schemes.

During the Thatcher years public housing provision declined as
council housing was sold off to the private sector. Responsibility for
new building passed to housing associations, which were inevitably
drawn to standardised projects with low capital costs and tending
toward sameness, and housing layouts, especially on estates, were
increasingly influenced by the requirements of the Highways
Department. Politicians rarely supported good design.

Postwar commercial architecture

The prefabricated concrete systems developed for high-rise mass
housing were equally suitable for office blocks, which came to London with a vengeance after the abolition of Building Licences in
1954. An early concrete-frame was the Economist Building, London
(1960-4, Alison and Peter Smithson). This coincided with the Post
Office Tower, London, 619 feet high (Sir Eric Bedford), with its
revolving restaurant and dramatic silhouette. London's skyline thus

punctured, a flood followed. Centre Point (1961-8, Richard Seifert) reached 121 metres. Its massive concrete piers and innovative 'pop' precast panels were an early example of fast-track construction. Many commercial towers followed: the Shell Centre, near Waterloo, the Vickers Tower at Millbank; the Hilton Hotel, Park Lane. Amongst the most depressing were the grim Marsham Street Towers of the Department of the Environment and the canyon of Victoria Street. Concrete and steel frames were clad with gridded glazing systems looking like graph paper, but glazing became increasingly sleek and sophisticated, a landmark being the Commercial Union tower (1969, Gollins Melvin Ward). Much commercial architecture was inevitably speculative and therefore bland; expensive materials such as polished granite cladding were frequently specified on otherwise mundane buildings.

There were a number of bitter wrangles such as Peter Palumbo's doomed attempt to raise a Mies van der Rohe designed glass tower in Mansion House Square, the saga of Paternoster Square and a battle for permission to erect a fine design by James Stirling at No. 1 Poultry, strongly opposed by Save Britain's Heritage. The completion of Canary Wharf (1992, Cesar Pelli) coincided with an economic slump. That sculptural shiny tower contains little architecture; it is mostly speculative open-plan office space and services.

The best architecture in the commercial sector showed variety, concern for location, increasing richness of form and texture and innovation in the mixing of old and new techniques and materials. The spectacularly refurbished Liverpool Street Station and Broadgate combined dramatic office accommodation looking over a central atrium with public external space including an arena. Highly sophisticated office buildings at Stockley Park near Heathrow went up only shortly before Richmond House, Whitehall, by William Whitfield, with its stone and brick banding and great mullioned and transomed oriel windows. Ralph Erskine's Ark (1992) is a spectacular creation, its glazed, outward-leaning walls a hull rising from the murk of Hammersmith to towers and galleries piercing the roof, the materials including extensive timber and copper. Other noteworthy offices are those by Edward Cullinan at Chilworth, Hampshire, and at Egham, Surrey, for Ready Mixed Concrete.

By such standards are judged many of the look-alike 1990s shopping centres, offices and public buildings, which have often used patterned brickwork and pitched tiled roofs as folksy covering to render contrived and sterile designs inoffensive.

The conservation movement and adaptation of existing buildings

There was a massive loss of Britain's built heritage in the first fifty years of the twentieth century. Country houses were abandoned, burnt down and blown up (one thousand destroyed in whole or part

51. *Castle Drogo, Devon, 1910-30; a refined, mature and powerful composition in granite – a private house by Sir Edwin Lutyens.*

52. *King George's Road, Port Sunlight, Merseyside; one of many diverse house designs displayed in this model village founded by the industrialist W.H. Lever, built from 1888.*

53. The Pier Head, Liverpool, with the Cunard Building (right), a reinforced concrete frame by Willink & Thicknesse (1913 onwards), and (left) the Liver Building, 1908-10, by Aubrey Thomas, another early example of a concrete frame.

54. The Penguin Pool, London Zoo, 1935, Berthold Lubetkin and Tecton; technical innovations of the time made possible slender interlocking concrete spiral ramps to show off the penguins.

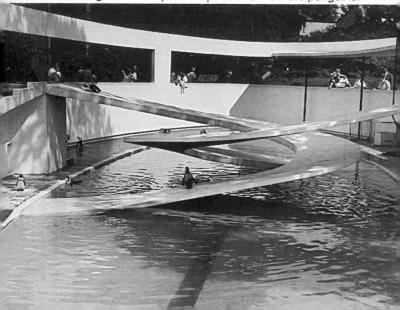

55. Portmeirion, Gwynedd, Wales, 1920-66; Italian stage-set architecture by Clough Williams-Ellis combining fragments of real buildings, whimsy and trompes l'oeil.

56. *BBC Broadcasting House, London, 1931, G.Val Myers; bringing great presence to a difficult site, the monolithic façade is modulated with Georgian window proportions and reliefs by Eric Gill. Unfortunately the fine interior no longer survives.*

57. Harlow, Essex: one of the first of the postwar New Towns. Coherent modern town planning based on mixed development principles.

58. The Metropolitan Cathedral of Christ the King, Liverpool: a high-crowned tent-like structure of concrete and glass enclosing the vast space of a centralised plan serving contemporary liturgical needs.

59. *Coventry Cathedral, 1951-62, Sir Basil Spence; tapering concrete columns support a modern vaulted roof enclosing a space richly decorated with fashionable contemporary design, blending art and architecture.*

60. The Barbican, London, 1957-81, Chamberlin, Powell & Bon;
identifiable if impersonal high-rise and low-rise dense housing
with abundant facilities laid out around piazzas, water features
and an Arts Centre.

61. *Royal National Theatre, London, 1967-76; Sir Denys Lasdun's angular use of concrete provides powerful sculpture at a distance and rich surface texture close by.*

62. *History Faculty, Cambridge University, 1964-9, Sir James Stirling; one of an early but influential trio of powerfully geometric compositions contrasting light patent glazing against hard masonry forms.*

63. Social housing, 1975-80, at St Mark's Road, London, for Kensington Housing Trust. Each 'house' is two narrow houses over a flat, all on an angle to the street, described by the architects, Jeremy and Fenella Dixon, as 'eclecticism with an artistic eye'.

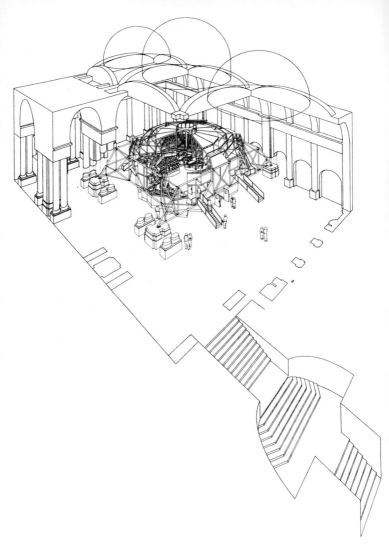

64. *Royal Exchange Theatre, Manchester, 1977; within the colossal but redundant Wool Hall Levitt Bernstein Associates suspended a new self-contained theatre capsule seating 450 people.*

65. *Bowra Building, Wadham College, Oxford University, MacCormac Jamieson & Pritchard; innovative student housing with a very English architectural pedigree.*

66. *Sainsbury Centre for the Arts, University of East Anglia, Norwich, 1977 (extended 1992), Sir Norman Foster. This cutaway section shows the part-glazed weatherproof skin carried over long span trusses, plus concealed service ducts.*

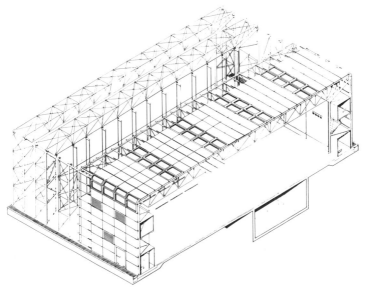

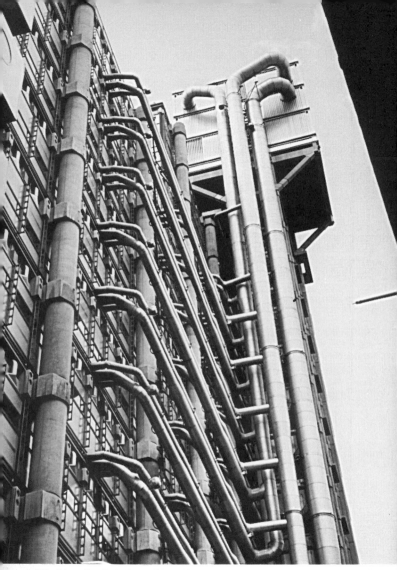

67. Lloyd's Building, City of London, 1981; Richard Rogers's controversial offices followed the success of his Pompidou Centre in Paris. Both projects are well-known for displaying their services externally.

68. *Princess of Wales Conservatory, Kew, 1988; simple contemporary sophistication is much more satisfying than would have been a pastiche of earlier forms.*

69. *Schlumberger Research Centre, Cambridge, 1985, Michael Hopkins; a visually strong lightweight building system of tensioned fabric steel supports and cables.*

70. *Northwood Tower, Waltham Forest, London. The 21-storey block was refurbished, strengthened and reclad on a rolling programme over eighteen months in the early 1990s, possible only through tenant participation with the architects, Hunt Thompson.*

71. *Gothick Villa, Regent's Park, London, 1990; Quinlan Terry's fluent Classicism shows the style to be a living language capable of beautiful proportions.*

72. *Stansted Airport Terminal, Essex, 1992, Sir Norman Foster; the beautifully lit roof above this disciplined, calming space is supported by a simple grid of lightweight tubular steel 'trees'.*

73. *Embankment Place, Charing Cross, London, 1991, Terry Farrell; the 'Air Rights' nine-storey office building soars over the railway station, providing a vigorous contemporary Post-modern frontage to the Thames.*

since 1908). Many fine interiors were gutted. In the 1950s acres of terracing were razed for new housing; even Georgian squares did not escape (Bloomsbury was bulldozed in 1959). Speculators bought historic properties to pull them down.

But the tide began to turn in the mid 1960s. The Landmark Trust was founded in 1965; the portico of the Tate Gallery was reprieved from demolition in 1968. A proposed rape of Bath (the 1950 development plan) was seen off in 1975 with only a few notable intruders. The conservation movement gained momentum with a host of successful rescues: Ironbridge Gorge; Barlaston Hall; Covent Garden; Billingsgate; Albert Dock, Liverpool. At long last a proper programme of long overdue maintenance and conservation was begun on historic buildings like the Houses of Parliament, castles, cathedrals, churches, country houses and the centres of historic towns.

Despite the efforts of architectural historians like Sir Nikolaus Pevsner and Sir John Summerson, architectural education and much of the establishment had in the 1960s turned their backs on the past and knowledge about the repair of old buildings was scarce. The revival of interest opened up a new area for architects and craftsmen, which resulted in a reassessment of traditional building techniques and materials. Whereas the new techniques of building tended to be brittle, exact, quick and of uncertain life, the old techniques were pliable, generally weathered better and were far more easily adaptable, not having been built to such critical limits in the first place. Old buildings needed gentle repair rather than notional restoration.

Some of the most successful projects involved a combination of repair and new work. One of the first was Edward Cullinan's Minster Lovell Mill Study Centre (1969), which reused drystone walling in a new building along traditional lines enlivened with contemporary details. They followed this with a variety of fascinating projects linking the old and new, such as Fountains Visitor Centre (1992), with its unusual curved roof and intimate scale. In Manchester, a self-contained steel and glass auditorium for the Royal Exchange Theatre was inserted into the vast former Wool Hall.

Despite the success of these schemes the public reaction to many of the worst buildings of the 1960s had been so profound that a groundswell of opinion turned against contemporary architecture. The Prince of Wales spoke for many when he likened a proposed extension to the National Gallery to 'a monstrous carbuncle on the face of a much loved friend', provoking uproar in the architectural establishment. Confidence slipped, and many who commisssioned buildings lost their nerve, seeking unsuccessfully to copy the past.

Education and culture

It was claimed that Britain led Europe in the 1950s with the best industrial systems and techniques suitable for national recovery.

Schools were a good example, spurred on by the 1944 Education Act, best shown in Hertfordshire, where a panel system provided airy lightweight steel-column and wall buildings which could be standardised for flexibility and distributed through regional depots. The result was so successful that nearly two hundred schools were erected in fifteen years. Further systems evolved, particularly CLASP (Consortium of Local Authorities Schools Programmes). A group of counties, led by Nottinghamshire, combined their demand in order to develop an economic prefabricated school-building system suitable for assembly by any builder on sites where subsidence could occur. This system was quick, cheap to erect, and popular.

The Smithsons took the idea behind the system to its architectural limit at Hunstanton School, 1953, a stark ascetic essay in yellow brick exposed on a black steel frame. Although the ruthless sophisticated factory aesthetic had more to do with ideas of rationalism and sculptural precision than the needs of schoolchildren, it had far greater intellectual integrity than, for example, the buildings associated with the Festival of Britain on London's South Bank (1951), whose aim was to direct public attention away from the bomb-scarred banks of the Thames to a more prosperous future. The centrepiece was the extensively glazed Royal Festival Hall (1951), followed by the Queen Elizabeth Hall, the Purcell Room and later the Haywood Gallery. This group of buildings is a testimony to the period, a brave experiment with the new material of concrete, new shapes and new structural forms and a degree of readiness to build up elements from preformed accessories. These buildings were interlinked with terraces and footbridges and raised circulation paths reminiscent of contemporary deck access housing systems of the time, for example in Coventry City Centre (1961) or the concrete ziggurats at the University of East Anglia (1963, Denys Lasdun). The South Bank complex was completed by Sir Denys Lasdun's National Theatre (1967-76), the most sublime of the buildings there: it is deep space architecture, with interlocking planes and stratified layers formed with galleries hung over voids. Many characteristics of concrete are on show: the rich texture and sculptural forms of shuttered mass concrete, the slender columns, the rigid geometry of waffle slabs.

University building commissions of the 1960s and 1970s provided a rich crop of architecture, generally, and not surprisingly, far more sophisticated than the building systems in use elsewhere. At Oxford, Arne Jacobsen's designs for St Catherine's College included the cutlery. The most striking results came from the office of James Stirling (1926-92), who produced three strikingly geometric university buildings made from red brick, reinforced concrete and industrial patent glazing: the Faculty of Engineering at Leicester (1959-63, with James Gowan), attacked by Sir Nikolaus Pevsner as 'actively ugly'; the History Library at Cambridge (1964-9) and the Florey Building at Oxford (1971). They brought an entirely new architectural vocabulary of geometric form, wit and spatial fluency to England. Many subsequent commissions, with Michael Wilford, were in Germany (Staatsgalerie, Stuttgart, 1977-84) and the USA (Rice University). It is ironic that his work in London remains restricted to the Clore Gallery extension to the Tate Gallery (1987) and proposals for Number 1 Poultry. Yet, after Lutyens, Stirling was probably the most influential architect of the twentieth century.

In the 1980s notable university commissions, although fewer, included MacCormac Jamieson and Pritchard's work at Oxford (Bowra Building, Wadham College, St John's College) and Cambridge (Blue Boar Court), which drew intellectually on English tradition. A combination of courtyards, loggias, sequential framed views, the penetration of daylight and good neighbourliness evoke a particular sensibility in these projects, leading Richard MacCormac, it is said, to the interesting assertion that from Robert Smythson to James Stirling, the 'best British building has often been a wilful misunderstanding of Classicism, tending to recur towards the end of each century.'

During the 1980s a new generation of schools was produced in Hampshire under the County Architects Department headed by Colin Stansfield-Smith, of which Hatch Warren Junior, Basingstoke, is a prime example. Its S-shaped plan echoes the rolling downland of the adjacent countryside, pitched and glazed roofs providing dramatic yet domestic-scaled internal space.

Buildings are cultural symbols, representing the aspirations of their time. A good example is Coventry Cathedral, destroyed by bombing in 1940 and rebuilt in 1962 to Sir Basil Spence's design. In poignant contrast to the scarred old walls stands a brave new concrete structure on slender columns brought to ground on brass pins. The new building is clearly of the 1960s, but its architectural consistency gives it a timeless quality. The Metropolitan Cathedral of Christ the King, Liverpool (1967, Frederick Gibberd), also has fine stained glass and imagery of the Crown of Thorns. But from the outside its shape has been misinterpreted as a 'funnel' or 'wigwam' and short-life materials (lowering the initial cost) have already begun to fail. One of the most recent cathedrals, Brentwood (Quinlan Terry), is a finely crafted essay in Classicism built in traditional materials which, it could be argued, owes nothing to postwar Britain.

Recent architecture: high-tech

Forward-looking architecture necessarily makes full use of the technology of the day and the combined skills of architect and engineer. The most successful results have a lightness, delicacy and rigorous consistency, combined with an air of efficiency, optimism about the future and at times playfulness. An early example is the angular steel and mesh Aviary at London Zoo (1962, Cedric Price, Lord Snowdon and engineer Frank Newby). The more laid-back

Reliance Controls Factory, Swindon (1967, Team 4 comprising Richard and Su Rogers and Norman and Wendy Foster) was a simple steel-framed building with exposed cross-bracing so precisely crafted as to be self-conscious. In a less pure form, the steel-framed shed proliferated over industrial estates throughout England. Norman Foster's Willis Faber Dumas Building, Ipswich (1975), received national acclaim. Dark-glass perimeter walls follow a piano-shaped plan reflecting the surrounding buildings by day and glowing to reveal its contents at night. Offices are open-planned around a central escalator route leading up to roof gardens of box-hedged turf. The Sainsbury Centre for the Arts, near Norwich (1977), followed, looking more like an industrial artefact than a conventional building, a precise assembly of welded tubular prismatic trusses giving a column-free art gallery 133 metres long, wrapped around with aluminium cladding, the glazed ends orientating open views over surrounding parkland; light levels to the assembled art works are controlled by motorised louvres giving the feel of a spaceship, which extends to the dramatic 1992 extension built largely below ground, the principal lake-viewing elevation being a dramatic curved windscreen of glass. At Stansted Airport Terminal Building, Foster's design relied on structural steel 'trees' supporting a lightweight roof admitting natural daylight without any glare. Each 'tree' integrates air handling, flight information, signs, clocks, lighting and so on.

The high-tech aesthetic so successfully and precisely pursued by Norman Foster inspired other English architects. A variety of techniques was developed, including the use of suspension cables, for example at Richard Rogers's sophisticated Inmos Microprocessor Factory at Newport (1982), where a structural H-frame — an 'exoskeleton'— holds together a system of exposed ducts, and at the Schlumberger Research Centre, Cambridge (1986, Michael Hopkins), where masts and cables support a translucent fabric. A similar feeling is evoked at Michael Hopkins's new stand at Lord's Cricket Ground, at his own steel and glass Hampstead House (1978), and the David Mellor Cutlery Factory, a great masonry drum below a lightweight conical roof.

Richard Rogers's controversial Lloyd's Building, London, is a high-tech essay in stainless steel over a concrete frame, a building produced in deep consultation with Lloyd's commissioning body. It is designed for expansion, growth, variation, replacement; the offices are laid out looking over a full-height atrium. Escalators, toilet pods and services are added in such a way that they can be unplugged and renewed as technology moves forward.

Other examples of high-tech include Nicholas Grimshaw's showcase newspaper buildings for the *Financial Times* and the *Western Morning News*, where everything is on display to the outside world through walls of planar glass on fin-like columns, and his Waterloo

International Terminal (1993), a 400 metre long four-level building of three-pinned asymmetric arches weaving a snake-like path along existing railway tracks, its blue steel external structure weatherproofed with 2500 glass panels and 13,000 stainless steel sheets.

In the 1980s a breakaway strand of architecture, 'Post-modernism', turned to flirtation with the symbols but not necessarily the content of previous ages. Thus a pediment from one source might be added to fenestration from a completely different building tradition and both of them used to face an unrelated plan form. The result was often theatrical, kitsch, individualistic, entertaining. It could also be serious, bringing fresh new forms and variety well suited to England's diverse construction industry. Terry Farrell contributed a number of examples in London, including Embankment Place. Architectural critics soon identified another trend, again related to literary criticism: deconstructivist buildings were all about intersecting planes, confusion and uncertainty; walls ceased to be vertical; the buildings spoke of alienation. Few buildings of this type were erected in England, but it indirectly influenced a number of projects.

Concern about links between legionnaires' disease and air conditioning systems, together with growing energy costs, encouraged a move back to natural ventilation and 'greener' buildings in the later 1980s. Buildings began to be thought of in terms of their total energy requirement, and capital costs set against larger long-term gains. One building that looked forward in this way was St Mary's Hospital, Isle of Wight, where Ahrends, Burton and Koralek broke down a normally characterless hospital into a series of landscaped courts, finishing much of the building in stainless steel for longevity, the interiors being designed to uplift the spirits of patients. Another was the temporary Expo 92 British Pavilion in Seville by Nicholas Grimshaw; here the sun's rays were transformed through solar collectors into power to supply a waterfall running continuously over the building's façade to keep it cool.

Architecture is not restricted to prestigious buildings; it certainly is not something 'added on'. The best English architecture has always had a quality which delights, each occasion being the unique response by the architect and client to a particular interplay of practical requirements: suitable materials, available site, orientation, services, statutory controls, contemporary technology and cost. Standardised solutions are mere building. Good design, uncompromised and resolved, has a timeless, satisfying and spiritually uplifting quality, evident as clearly in domestic projects and shop interiors as in the architecture of national importance described in this book. As society changes, so do its buildings; they tend to reflect cultural values and concerns and record them for future generations. Let enlightened patrons continue to commission good, creative English architecture, arguably the best in the world.

Glossary of terms

Abutment: solid masonry resisting lateral pressure.

Acanthus: conventionalised leaf in Classical decoration.

Aesthetic: relation to the perception of beauty.

Aesthetics: philosophy of art.

Aisle: lower division of a church or basilica parallel to the higher nave, choir or transept, from which it is divided by pillars.

Alure: passage behind a parapet.

Ambulatory: aisle round an apse or circular building or across the east end of a church.

Amphitheatre: an oval or elliptical building with an arena surrounded by tiers of seats.

Apse: semicircular or polygonal end of a church or side chapel.

Arcade: sequence of arches on columns or pillars.

Architrave: bottom member of an entablature.

Art Nouveau: the movement flourished 1890-1914 in France, Belgium, Vienna and to a limited extent in Britain. Buildings have flowing, sinuous lines often incorporating decorative iron and coloured glass inspired by geometric and floral patterns.

Atrium: in Roman architecture an enclosed inner court; a forecourt in early Christian and Byzantine churches; in post-1970 office blocks and hotels a giant light well, often the full height of a tall building, providing a central feature and circulation space.

Attic: low storey above a main cornice.

Bailey: external wall or internal court of a castle.

Balustrade: row of balusters supporting a coping.

Barbican: outwork or detached feature protecting the approach to a castle.

Barge-boarding: inclined boards, often ornamented, fixed over the verge of a gable.

Baroque: stylistic (and Catholic) term dating from sixteenth-century Italy. Buildings are spectacular, characterised by a feeling of controlled but continuous geometric movement and a free blending of architecture, painting and sculpture.

Barrel-vault: arched stone covering running the length of a building and unbroken by cross-vaults.

Basilica: hall or church with aisles and a nave higher than the aisles.

Batter: slight inward inclination of a wall from the base upwards.

Bay: vertical unit of a wall or façade; also compartment of a nave.

Berm: ledge between ditch and parapet base in fortification.

Blind storey: triforium.

Boss: keystone at the intersection of vault ribs.

Broach: half-pyramid of masonry joining an octagonal spire to a square tower.

Brutalism: stylistic term referring to the French *beton brut,* literally rough undecorated concrete purposely unconcealed by applied decoration.

Burh: Anglo-Saxon fortified place, a town.

Buttress: projecting vertical mass of masonry resisting an outward thrust or stiffening a wall. **Flying buttress:** an arched prop of masonry resisting the lateral pressure of a wall.

Calefactory: warming room in a monastery.

Cantilever: projecting beam held down at the wall end by the superincumbent weight or in some other way.

Capital: moulded or carved top of a column.

Caryatid: sculptured female figure used as a support.

Castellum: small Roman fort of about 5 acres (2 hectares).

Cella: central portion of a Roman temple.

Chamfer: bevelled edge.

Chancel: eastern part of a church reserved for clergy and choir.

Channelling: grooving on a surface.

Chapter house: where the governing body of a monastery or cathedral meets.

Chevet: eastern termination of a church formed by an apse surrounded by an aisle off which chapels open.

Choir: portion of a church set aside for clergy and choir, divided off from the rest by a screen.

Cladding: thin external weatherproof wall covering, bearing no load.

Classicism: stylistic term relating to architecture derived from the Classical Orders (Doric, Ionic and Corinthian) of the ancient world and obeying certain rules of proportion and composition.

Clerestory: upper part of a nave with windows above the aisle roof.

Cloister: covered walk in a monastery or college, usually arranged round the sides of a square grass plot or 'garth'.

Cob: mixture of clay and chopped straw formerly used for walling in some rural areas.

Coffering: panels sunk deeply into the surface of a ceiling.

Cold-bridging: a building element which conducts coldness from outside through an insulated wall, risking condensation.

Coping: constructional term, usually a brick or concrete capping overhanging (and thereby protecting) the top of an external wall.

Corbel: projecting brick, tile or masonry bracket.

Corbelling: a series of corbels extending progressively further forward, one above the other.

Cornice: projecting upper portion of an entablature or any projecting top course.

Corps de logis: principal block at the centre of a great Renaissance house with spreading symmetrical wings.

Cottage orné: sophisticated Regency cottage deliberately designed to appear picturesque and quaint, typically by using rustic materials.

Cove: broad concave moulding between a ceiling and a wall.

Crenellation: battlements.

Crocket: curved, leaf-like ornament in Gothic architecture.

Crucks (cricks): curved main timbers used in timber-framed construction.

Culvert: underground channel.

Curtain wall: wall between two towers or bastions in fortification. In contemporary architecture **curtain walling** is another term for 'cladding'.

Cusp: point between the small arcs of trefoil and quatrefoil tracery.

Dais: platform at the end of a hall.

Deconstructivism: style where buildings are fragmented and built up in layers, frequently leaning at disconcerting angles.

Diaper: geometrical or floral surface pattern.

Dome: convex roof, approximately hemispherical. A **saucer dome** has a flat curve.

Domus: Roman town house.

Donjon: castle keep.

Dorter: sleeping quarters of a monastery.

Dressings: blocks of smooth stone used as quoins or frames for doors or windows.

Dripstone: projecting moulding to throw off rainwater from openings.

Drum: circular or polygonal structure on which a dome is raised.

Eclectic: of a style selecting elements from a variety of sources.

Embrasure: open portion of a battlement.

Entablature: horizontal top part of a Classical order. It consists of architrave, frieze and cornice and is supported by columns.

Expressionism: the movement flourished in the early 1920s, especially in Germany. Buildings are very sculptural with swooping, curved roofs, and unnaturally strong, exaggerated forms, sometimes anthropomorphic.

Façade: face or front of a building.

Fanlight: oblong or semicircular light over a door.

Fenestration: arrangement of windows in a façade.

Finial: ornamental top part of a spire or pinnacle.

Fluting: vertical channelling on the shaft of a column.

Footings: projecting courses at the base of a wall.

Forebuilding: structure protecting the entrance to a keep.

Forum: central open space in a Roman town, surrounded by public buildings.

Fosse: wet or dry ditch or moat, the upcast forming a rampart.

Frame construction: construction where loads are carried entirely by vertical stanchions and horizontal girders of steel, reinforced concrete or timber.

Frater: refectory of a monastery.

Frieze: middle member of an entablature or, in a room, space between top of the panelling and the cornice or ceiling.

Gable: vertical, triangular portion of a wall at the end of a ridged roof.

Gablet: little gable on a buttress.

Gallery: another name for the tribune.

Galleting: constructional term for small stones let into the joints of rubble walls, providing decoration and a good key.

Garderobe: privy in the wall of a castle.

Geodesic dome: regular geometric dome constructed from short steel rods interconnected at the nodes to provide a large span uninterrupted by tie-bars.

Greek cross: cross with all four arms of equal length.

Groin: edge formed by intersecting vaults.

Herm: quadrangular pillar broadening upwards and surmounted by a head or bust, popular in landscape gardens and with Robert Adam.

Hotel: large French town house.

Hypocaust: chamber below ground level heated by hot air from a furnace. Roman system of heating a building or important room.

Insula: Roman tenement-like living block.

Jamb: vertical part of the masonry of a door or window.

Jetty: overhanging storey, found mainly in timber-frame construction.

Keep: inner tower of a castle, usually the principal one.

Label: see *Dripstone*.

Lancet: tall narrow window with a sharply pointed head.

Lantern: small structure, open or glazed, crowning a dome or roof.

Latin cross: cross with one of the four arms elongated.

Lierne: decorative rib in a Gothic vault which does not spring from the wall or touch the central boss.

Light: division of a window.

Locutorium: room in a monastery where conversation was permitted for certain purposes.

Loggia: covered gallery behind an open arcade or colonnade.

Loop: 'arrow-slit' in fortification.

Louvre: ventilator in a roof or wall, usually slatted.

Machicolations: floor openings in a stone parapet.

Mannerism: the movement began in the Renaissance when architects such as Michelangelo and Romano began to use Classical elements in a manner which was not traditional. This could be intellectually disturbing, suggesting structural instability to the uninitiated: buildings which are not what they seem.

Mansard roof: a roof sloping at two distinct angles, a steep lower slope and flattish upper slope, giving additional floorspace.

Mausoleum: magnificent tomb.

Megalithic: made of large stones.

Merlon: solid portion of a battlement.

Metope: panel between triglyphs.

Modulor: system of measurement used in design, invented by Le Corbusier, combining the proportions of the human body with the Golden Section – a Platonically perfect geometric shape.

Module: measure of proportion by which the parts of a Classical building are regulated; in modern practice a convenient unit upon which all the dimensions of a building and its components are based for economy and ease of construction.

Motte: mound on which the wooden tower of an early Norman castle was built.

Moulding: continuous ornamental lines of grooving or projections.

Mullion: vertical division between lights of a window.

Narthex: porch in front of the nave and aisles of a church.

Nave: central division of a church west of the chancel arch or crossing, with or without side aisles.

Neo-classicism: the movement was a reaction in the later eighteenth century to the excesses of baroque and rococo, and to discoveries about ancient Greece and Rome. Typically, buildings are clean and uncluttered with simple elegant decoration.

Niche: ornamental recess in a wall.

Nogging: brickwork in a timber frame.

Obelisk: tall, tapering, square shaft.

Offset: sloping ledge on a buttress at the recession of a stage.

Ogee: arch of double curvature; first convex, then concave.

Order: in Classical architecture, a column (consisting of base, shaft, and capital) with the entablature it supports. In medieval architecture, a ring of voussoirs in an arch.

Oriel: window projecting from a wall surface by corbelling.

Overdoor: small pediment over a door.

Palladian: stylistic term relating to Andrea Palladio, the Italian High Renaissance architect , who was particularly influential in England.

Pargeting: exterior plasterwork, usually patterned.

Pavilion: projecting feature at the end of a Classical façade or ornamental building, usually self-contained and symmetrical.

Pediment: triangular end of the moderately pitched roof of a Classical building, above the top of the entablature or cornice; similar form used over door or window openings, sometimes segmental.

Pele tower: border keep, usually sixteenth-century.

Pent-roofed: with a lean-to roof.

Peristyle: colonnade round a building or courtyard.

Piano nobile: principal floor of a large house raised one storey above ground level.

Piazza: formal open space or square surrounded by buildings in a town.

Pier: solid support of a pair of arches of an arcade.

Pilaster: rectangular column usually engaged with the wall but projecting from it.

Piloti: stylised columns used to raise a Modernist building on legs above the ground, favoured by Le Corbusier.

Pinnacle: tapering termination of a vertical form.

Pitch: inclination of a roof.

Planar glazing: frameless silicone jointed self-supporting glass walls braced with glass fins, used increasingly since the late 1970s.

Plinth: projecting base of a building or column.

Podium: platform on which a building is raised or lowest stage of a column pedestal.

Portico: roofed space, open on at least one side, and enclosed by a range of columns supporting the roof.

Porticus: north or south porch of a Saxon church.

Postern: concealed exit from a castle; a sally-port.

Post-modernism: movement flourishing in the 1980s as a reaction to the monotony of contemporary architecture. It seeks fun, wit, surface decoration, colour and sometimes quotes light-heartedly from the history of architecture.

Prefabrication: manufacture of components beforehand for assembly on site.

Presbytery: eastern part of the chancel beyond the choir.

Quatrefoil: circular or square opening having four 'foils' separated by 'cusps'. A **trefoil** has three foils.

Quoins: corner stones at the angle of a building.

Refectory: communal dining-hall.

Reinforced concrete (ferro-concrete): concrete whose tensile strength has been greatly increased by embedding steel rods and mesh in it .

Respond: half-pillar attached to a wall and supporting an arch.

Rib: stone arch on the groin or surface of a vault.

Rococo: an extension of the baroque with less attention to the Classical Orders; more precious, intricate and richly decorated. At its most extreme in Austria and southern Germany.

Roundel: decorative disc or medallion.

Rustication: stonework of large freestone blocks (rough or smooth) with recessed joints.

Shell structure: dome, vault or other geometric shape formed in thin, self-supporting concrete.

Solar: medieval chamber on an upper floor.

Space-frame: framework of short steel rods interconnected at the nodes to roof large spans without tie-rods.

Spandrel: triangular space between the curve of an arch and a rectangle enclosing it.

Springers: lower stones of an arch or vault.

Spur: projecting stonework at the base of an angle designed to protect it.

Strapwork: ornament composed of interlacing bands or straps.

String-course: projecting horizontal band along a wall.

Stucco: plaster applied to a wall or ceiling surface; usually moulded decoratively when used internally or smoothed and painted externally.

Suspended ceiling: system of prefabricated, easily changed components designed to be hung from a more permanent structure.

Swag: festoon of fruit, flowers and foliage.

Terracotta: burnt-clay product harder than brick.

Tessellated: of flooring made of mosaic.

Tesserae: cubes of mosaic.

Tierceron: rib of a Gothic vault inserted between the transverse and diagonal ribs.

Tile hanging: overlapping tiles hung vertically.

Tracery: intersecting bars of moulded stone forming patterns in Gothic windows.

Transept: either arm of the tranverse part of a cruciform church.

Transom: horizontal division between the lights of a window.

Trefoil: see *Quatrefoil.*

Tribune: corridor above the aisles with open arches to the nave.

Triforium: space formed between the aisle roof and the aisle vault.

Triglyph: vertical grooved member of a Doric frieze.

Trombe wall: glass wall designed to catch the heat of the sun and passively heat a building.

Trompe l'oeil: wall-painted image which pretends to be real, such as a door, window etc.

Tympanum: space between the lintel and an arch above.

Undercroft: vaulted basement.

Vallum: rampart.

Vault: arched covering of stone.

Vernacular architecture: building in the native provincial idiom unaffected by fashionable or learned taste.

Villa: Roman country house, later a detached suburban house.

Volute: scroll.

Voussoir: wedge-shaped block forming part of an arch.

Wagon roof: an arched braced roof lined with boarding.

Wainscoting: covering of walls with boards of wood.

Wattle and daub: vertical covering of interlacing twigs (or 'wattles') plastered with clay (or 'daub').

Weather-boarding: exterior covering of overlapping, horizontal boards.

Web: panel of a vault.

Gazetteer of representative buildings

Prehistoric
Neolithic chambered long barrows: Hetty Pegler's Tump, Uley, Glos; Stoney Littleton, Radstock, Avon.
Bronze age temple: Stonehenge, Amesbury, Wilts.
Bronze age hut settlement: Kestor, Chagford, Devon.
Iron age hillfort: Maiden Castle, Dorchester, Dorset.
Iron age fortifications: Stanwick, N. Yorks.
Iron age and Romano-British village: Chysauster, Trevarrack, Cornwall.

Roman
Town site, forum, houses, theatre: Verulamium, St Albans, Herts.
Town site with basilica and public baths: Viroconium, Wroxeter, Shropshire; Calleva Atrebatum, Silchester, Hants.
Military base and settlement: Corstopitum, Corbridge, Northumb.
Fort and sections of Hadrian's Wall: Borcovicium, Housesteads, Northumb.
Public baths: Aquae Sulis, Bath, Avon.
Villas: Chedworth, Glos; Bignor and Fishbourne, W. Sussex; Lullingstone, Kent.
Coastal fort: Burgh Castle, Great Yarmouth, Norfolk; Richborough, Kent.
Signal station: Scarborough, N. Yorks.

Anglo-Saxon
Seventh-century churches: St Pancras, Canterbury, Kent; Brixworth, Northants; Monkwearmouth and Jarrow, Tyne & Wear; Escomb, Durham; crypt at Repton, Derbys.
Eighth-century: Offa's Dyke; crypts at Hexham, Northumb, and Ripon Minster, N. Yorks.
Ninth-century church: Britford, Wilts.
Tenth-century churches: Deerhurst, Glos; Bradford-on-Avon, Wilts; Wing, Bucks; Worth, W.Sussex; Breamore, Hants; Clapham, Beds; Earl's Barton, Northants; Wittering, Cambs.
Eleventh-century churches: Stow, Lincs; Bosham and Sompting, W. Sussex; Greensted, Essex; foundations of St Augustine's Abbey, Canterbury; remains of cathedral at North Elmham, Norfolk.

Anglo-Norman
Work at the cathedrals of Durham; Winchester; Hereford; Oxford; Norwich; Chichester; Ely; Gloucester; Peterborough, Rochester; St Albans; Southwell; Worcester (crypt).
Abbeys: Tewkesbury, Glos; Waltham Abbey, Essex; Malmesbury,

Wilts; Bury St Edmunds, Suffolk; Furness, Cumbria; Kirkstall, W. Yorks; Romsey, Hants.

Priories: Castle Acre, Norfolk; Blyth, Notts; Christchurch, Dorset.

Parish churches at Adel, W. Yorks; Lastingham, N. Yorks; St John the Baptist, Chester; Kilpeck, Herefs; Barfreston, Kent; Iffley, Oxon; Melbourne, Derbys; Stewkley, Bucks; Studland, Dorset; Elkstone, Glos; St Sepulchre and St Peter, Northampton; Castor, Cambs; Walsoken, Norfolk; St Bartholomew the Great, London.

Castles: Berkhamsted, Herts; Restormel and Trematon, Cornwall; Rochester and Dover, Kent; Orford, Suffolk; Keep of the Tower of London (with the Chapel of St John); Colchester and Castle Hedingham, Essex; Castle Rising, Norfolk; Carlisle, Cumbria; Richmond, Helmsley and Scarborough, N. Yorks; Conisbrough, S. Yorks.

Manor houses at Burton Agnes, Humberside; Boothby Pagnell, Lincs; Aaron the Jew's House and St Mary's Guild, Lincoln; Merchant's Houses, Bury St Edmunds, Suffolk, and Southampton; eleventh-century Scolland's Hall, Richmond Castle, N. Yorks; twelfth-century halls at Oakham, Leics, and Bishop's Hall, Hereford.

Early English

Work at the cathedrals of Canterbury; Salisbury; Lincoln; Wells; Worcester; York; Ripon; Southwark; Southwell; and Beverley Minster.

Abbeys: Westminster; Roche, S. Yorks; Rievaulx, Fountains and Whitby, N. Yorks; Tintern, Gwent.

Priories: Hexham, Northumb; Tynemouth, Tyne & Wear; Finchale, Durham.

Parish churches: Ketton and Empingham, Leics; Raunds and Warmington, Northants; Newark on Trent, Notts; Threekingham, Lincs; Cherry Hinton, Cambs; West Walton and Blakeney, Norfolk; Chipstead and Ockham, Surrey; Abbey Dore, Herefs; Whitchurch Canonicorum, Dorset; Darlington and St Andrew Auckland, Durham; Haltwhistle, Northumb; Stone, Kent.

Castles: Flint and Rhuddlan, Clwyd; Kidwelly and Pembroke, Dyfed; Chepstow, Gwent; Beaumaris, Caernarvon, Conway and Harlech, Gwynedd; Corfe Castle, Dorset; Pevensey, E. Sussex; Goodrich, Herefs; Clifford's Tower, city walls and gateways, York; Framlingham, Suffolk.

Manor houses: Stokesay and Acton Burnell, Shropshire; Little Wenham, Suffolk; Charney Bassett, Oxon; Old Soar, Kent.

Merton College, Oxford.

Tithe barns at Bredon, Worcs; Great Coxwell, Oxon; Glastonbury Abbey, Somerset.

Town planning at (New) Winchelsea, E. Sussex.

Decorated

Work at the cathedrals of Exeter; Bristol; Lichfield; Lincoln; Ely;

York; Chester; Southwell; and Beverley Minster.

Abbeys: Westminster; Selby, N. Yorks; Tewkesbury, Glos; Tintern, Gwent; Milton, Dorset; Dorchester, Oxon; Malmesbury, Wilts.

Parish churches: Yaxley, Cambs; Ashbourne, Derbys; Winchelsea, E. Sussex; Ledbury, Herefs; Patrington and Holy Trinity, Hull, Humberside; Boston, Grantham, Heckington and St Mary, Stamford, Lincs; Cley, Norfolk; Rushden, Northants; Skipton, N. Yorks; Bloxham and Chipping Norton, Oxon; Melverley, Shropshire; Woolpit, Suffolk; Holy Trinity, Coventry; Otley and Wakefield (chantry chapel and bridge), W. Yorks.

Castles: Bodiam, E. Sussex; Warwick; Ludlow, Shropshire; Nunney, Somerset; Castle Bolton, N. Yorks; Lumley and Raby, Durham.

Manor houses: Penshurst Place, Kent; Haddon Hall, Derbys; Grevel's House, Chipping Campden, Glos; Markenfield and Spofforth, N. Yorks; Maxstoke, Warwicks.

Cruck cottage at Spilsby, Lincs.

Tithe barn at Bradford-on-Avon, Wilts.

Perpendicular

Work at the cathedrals of Canterbury; Winchester; Manchester; Gloucester; York; Worcester; and Beverley Minster.

Sherborne Abbey, Dorset; King's College Chapel, Cambridge; St George's Chapel, Windsor; Great Malvern Priory, Worcs; St Mary Redcliffe and St Stephen, Bristol; Prior's Lodging, Much Wenlock, Shropshire.

Parish churches: Chipping Campden, Northleach and Cirencester, Glos; Bruton and Wells, Somerset; Edington, Wilts; Launceston, Cornwall; Fotheringhay, Northants; Gedney and Louth, Lincs; St Nicholas, King's Lynn; Terrington St Clement, Walpole St Peter, Swaffham, Cawston and Sall, Norfolk; St Peter Mancroft, Norwich; March, Cambs; Long Melford, Lavenham, Needham Market, Blythburgh and Southwold, Suffolk; Ormskirk, Lancs; Hawkshead, Cumbria; Thirsk and Giggleswick, N. Yorks; Gawsworth and Lower Peover, Cheshire; Holy Trinity, Stratford-upon-Avon, Warwicks.

Castles: Herstmonceux, E. Sussex; Tattershall, Lincs; Warkworth and Dunstanburgh, Northumb; Raglan, Gwent.

Manor houses: Great Chalfield, Wilts; Wingfield, Derbys; Hoghton Tower, Lancs; Oxburgh Hall, Norfolk; Cothay and Lytes Cary, Somerset; Bradley, Devon; Cotehele, Cornwall; Ockwells, Berks; Great Dixter, E. Sussex.

Yeomen's houses: Stoneacre and Synyards, Otham, Kent; Bignor, W. Sussex; Giffords Hall and Lavenham Hall, Suffolk; Coggeshall, Essex.

Houses at Chiddingstone, Kent; Colston's, Bristol.

Cruck cottages at Didbrook, Glos, and Spilsby, Lincs.

Eton and Winchester Colleges; Queens' College, Cambridge; Lincoln College, Oxford.

Hospital and Grammar School, Ewelme, Oxon; Bede House Hospital, Stamford, Lincs.

Guildhalls at Cirencester, Glos, and Norwich; St George's Guildhall, King's Lynn, Norfolk; Guildhall and Merchant Adventurers' Hall, York; roof of Westminster Hall, London.

George Inn, Glastonbury, and George Inn, Norton St Philip, Somerset.

Tudor (1500 - 1600)

Henry VII's Chapel, Westminster; Bath Abbey, Avon; Nicholas West's Chapel, Ely, Cambs.

Deal Castle, Kent.

Country houses: Compton Wynyates and Coughton Court, Warwicks; East Barsham, Norfolk; Hengrave, Suffolk; Layer Marney Tower, Essex; Barrington Court, Somerset; Loseley Park, Surrey; Parham Park, W. Sussex; Breamore, Hants; Hampton Court Palace, London; Pitchford Hall, Shropshire; Speke, Merseyside; Rufford, Lancs; Bramall, Greater Manchester; Little Moreton, Cheshire; Sizergh and Levens, Cumbria.

Houses at York; Shrewsbury; Henley-in-Arden, Warwicks; Merchant's House, Nantwich, Cheshire.

Parish church: Standish, Gtr Manchester.

St John's College, Cambridge.

Guildhalls at Lavenham, Suffolk; Thaxted, Essex; Old Market Hall, Shrewsbury; Leycester's Hospital, Warwick.

Staples Inn, Holborn, London; The Feathers, Ludlow, Shropshire.

Elizabethan and Jacobean buildings (*c.*1550-1620)

Longleat, Wilts; Wollaton Hall, Notts; Hardwick Hall, Derbys; Burton Agnes, Humberside (Robert Smythson). Bolsover Castle, Derbys (John Smythson). Hatfield House, Herts; Blickling Hall, Norfolk (Robert Lyminge). Montacute House, Somerset; Castle Ashby, Northants; Staunton Harold Chapel, Leics; Stokesay Castle Gatehouse, Shropshire; Stanway, Glos; Little Moreton Hall, Cheshire; Audley End, Essex; Burghley House, Lincs; Caius College, Cambridge; Merton and Wadham Colleges, Oxford; Guildhall, Exeter; Charterhouse School, London.

Early English Baroque buildings (*c.*1619-1715).

The Banqueting House, Whitehall; Queen's House, Greenwich; St Paul's, Covent Garden (Inigo Jones). Kingston Lacy, Dorset (Sir Roger Pratt). Sheldonian Theatre, Oxford; St Paul's Cathedral; St Stephen's Walbrook and 51 churches, City of London; St James's, Piccadilly; Tom Tower, Oxford; Greenwich Hospital; Hampton Court; Trinity College, Cambridge (Sir Christopher Wren). Dyrham Park (Avon); Chatsworth House, Derbys (south front); Uppark, W. Sussex (William Talman). St Anne's, Limehouse; Christ Church, Spitalfields; St Mary

Woolnoth, London; Castle Howard Mausoleum, N. Yorks (Nicholas Hawksmoor). Castle Howard, N. Yorks; Blenheim Palace, Oxon; Seaton Delaval Hall, Northumb (Sir John Vanbrugh). Birmingham Cathedral; St Paul's, Deptford, and St John, Smith Square, London (Thomas Archer).

English Palladian and Georgian buildings (c.1720-1800)

Mereworth Castle, Kent; Stourhead, Wilts (Colen Campbell). St Martin-in-the-Fields, London; Radcliffe Library, Oxford (James Gibbs). Holkham Hall, Norfolk (with others); Stowe, Bucks; Horse Guards, Whitehall (William Kent). Chiswick House, London; Assembly Rooms, York (Lord Burlington). Palladian Bridge, Wilton House,Wilts (Roger Morris). Woburn Abbey, Beds (Henry Flitcroft). Prior Park and The Circus, Bath (John Wood the Elder). Shugborough, Staffs (James Athenian Stuart). Chinese Pagoda, Kew Gardens; Somerset House, London (Sir William Chambers). Royal Crescent and Assembly Rooms, Bath (John Wood the Younger). Syon House, Middx; Kenwood, Hampstead; Newby Hall, N. Yorks; Kedleston Hall, Derbys; Harewood House, W. Yorks (Robert Adam). Doddington Hall, Cheshire (Samuel Wyatt). St James, Great Packington, Warwicks (Joseph Bonomi). All Hallows, London Wall; Guildhall, London (George Dance). Chester Castle; The Lyceum, Liverpool (Thomas Harrison). Heveningham Hall, Suffolk (interior); Radcliffe Observatory, Oxford (James Wyatt). The Egyptian House, Penzance, Cornwall (John Foulston).

Regency and early nineteenth-century buildings (c.1800-37)

The Royal Pavilion, Brighton; Blaise Hamlet, Bristol; Regent's Park and Cumberland Terrace, London; All Souls', Langham Place, London (John Nash). Sezincote, Glos (S. P. Cockerell). Sir John Soane's Museum and Dulwich Art Gallery, London; Pell Wall House, Staffs; Wimpole Hall, Cambs (John Soane). Lansdown and Montpellier Estate and Rotunda, Cheltenham (John Papworth). Downing College, Cambridge; The Grange, Hants; National Gallery, London (William Wilkins). Eastnor Castle, Herefs; British Museum (Sir Robert Smirke). Royal Arcade, Newcastle upon Tyne (Grainger and Dobson). Much of Belgravia and Pimlico (Thomas Cubitt). Mamhead, Devon; Harlaxton Manor, Lincs (Anthony Salvin). St Katherine's Dock, London (Philip Hardwick). St Pancras New Church, London (Henry Inwood). Triple Archway, Hyde Park Corner (Decimus Burton).

Early Victorian buildings (c.1837-60)

Great Moreton Hall, Cheshire (Edward Blore). King's Cross Station, London; Osborne House, Isle of Wight (Thomas Cubitt). Taylorian [Ashmolean] Building, Oxford (C. R. Cockerell). Houses of Parliament (with Pugin) and Reform Club, Pall Mall, London; Cliveden,

Bucks (Sir Charles Barry). Palm House, Kew Gardens (Decimus Burton). Catholic cathedrals at Birmingham and Nottingham; Scarisbrick Hall, Lancs (A.W.N. Pugin). Shadwell Park, Norfolk; Elvetham Hall, Hants (Samuel Sanders Teulon). St George's Hall, Liverpool (Harvey L. Elmes). All Saints' Church, Margaret Street, London (William Butterfield). Albert Dock, Liverpool (Jesse Hartley). Mentmore Towers, Bucks; Crystal Palace (Joseph Paxton). Caledonian Road and St Vincent Street churches, Glasgow (Alexander Greek Thomson). Leeds Town Hall (Cuthbert Brodrick).

High Victorian buildings (c. 1860-1901)

Albert Memorial and St Pancras Station, London (Sir George Gilbert Scott). All Saints', Clifton, Bristol; Royal Courts of Justice, London (Edmund Street). Castell Coch, Cardiff (William Burges). Town Hall, Manchester; Natural History Museum, London (Alfred Waterhouse). Leighton House, Holland Park, London (George Aitchison). Cragside, Rothbury, Northumb; Bryanston, Dorset; New Scotland Yard, London (Richard Norman Shaw). 6 Ellerdale Road, Hampstead, London; Broadlands, Romsey, Hants (W.E. Nesfield). Oriel Chambers, Liverpool (Peter Ellis).

The Grand Manner and Edwardian buildings (c. 1889-1914)

British Museum, Edward VII Gallery, and Kodak House, Kingsway, London (Sir John Burnet). Prudential Assurance Buildings, London (Alfred Waterhouse). Institute of Chartered Accountants and Royal Insurance Building, London (John Belcher). War Office, Whitehall (William Young). Cardiff City Hall and Law Courts; Deptford Town Hall, London; Hull School of Art (Lanchester, Stewart & Rickards). Victoria and Albert Museum, Kensington; Royal Naval College, Dartmouth; Buckingham Palace Public Façade and The Mall, London (Sir Aston Webb). Library Wing of the Law Society, Chancery Lane, London (Charles Holden). Central Criminal Courts, Old Bailey, London; Lancaster Town Hall (Edward Mountford). County Hall, London (Ralph Knott). The Ritz and the RAC Club, London (Mewès & Davis). The Quadrant, Regent Street (Sir Reginald Blomfield).

Arts and Crafts and English Free School buildings (c. 1859-1939)

The Red House, Bexleyheath, Kent (Philip Webb). Holy Trinity Church, Sloane Street, London (J.D. Sedding). Westminster Cathedral, London (John Francis Bentley). Bishopsgate Institute; Whitechapel Art Gallery; Horniman Museum (all London, C. Harrison Townsend). 8 Addison Road, Kensington (Halsey Ricardo). Avon Tyrrell, Hants; All Saints' Church, Brockhampton (William Lethaby). Broadleys and Moor Crag, Cartmel Fell, Windermere, Cumbria; The Orchard, Chorleywood, Herts (C.F.A. Voysey). 37-9 and 72-4 Cheyne Walk, London (C.R. Ashbee). Glasgow School of Art; Hill House, Helensburgh, Strathclyde (Charles Rennie Mackintosh). Tigbourne

Court, Surrey; Deanery Garden, Sonning, Berks; Heathcote, Ilkley, W.Yorks; Castle Drogo, Devon; The Salutation, Sandwich, Kent; Cenotaph, Whitehall, London; Britannic House, Finsbury Circus; Gledstone Hall, Yorks; crypt, Liverpool (Catholic) Cathedral; Page Street Estate, Westminster; Midland Bank, Poultry, London (Sir Edwin Lutyens). Church of Christ Scientist, Manchester (Edgar Wood). Liverpool (Anglican) Cathedral (Sir Giles Gilbert Scott). Michelin Tyre Building, Fulham Road (F. Espinasse). Quarr Abbey, Isle of Wight (Dom Paul Bellot).

Modernism and inter-war buildings (c.1922-38)

London Transport HQ; Morden, Arnos Grove and Boston Manor Underground stations; Senate House (all London; Charles Holden). Battersea Power Station, London (Sir Giles Gilbert Scott). Royal Corinthian Yacht Club, Burnham-on-Crouch, Essex; Simpson's, Piccadilly (Joseph Emberton). Boots Factory, Beeston, Notts; Daily Express Building, Fleet Street (Sir Owen Williams). Highpoint 1 and 2, Hampstead, London; Gorilla House and Penguin Pool, London Zoo (Berthold Lubetkin). Port of London Authority Building (Sir Edwin Cooper). House at Willow Road, London (Ernö Goldfinger). Bush House, Aldwych, London (Helmle, Corbett & Harrison). Ideal/Palladium House, London (Raymond Hood & Gordon Jeeves). High and Over, Amersham, Bucks (Amyas Connell). City Hall, Swansea (Sir Percy Thomas). Cunard Building, Liverpool (Willinck & Thicknesse). St Nicholas Church, Burnage, Manchester (Cachemaille Day & Lander). Hay's Wharf and St Olave House, London (H. S. Goodhart-Rendel). Hoover Factory, Great West Road, London (Wallis Gilbert). Lawn Road Flats, Hampstead, London (Wells Coates). Royal Shakespeare Memorial Theatre, Stratford-upon-Avon, Warwicks (Elizabeth Scott). RIBA Building, Portland Place, London (Grey Wornurn). BBC Broadcasting House, London (G. Val Myer). De La Warr Pavilion, Bexhill, E. Sussex (Erich Mendelsohn & Serge Chermayeff). Guildford Cathedral (Sir Edward Maufe). Peter Jones Store, London (William Crabtree). Odeon, Carlton and Gaumont cinemas across London (George Coles).

Garden cities and new towns

Bedford Park Estate, Turnham Green, London, 1877 (Norman Shaw). Port Sunlight, Merseyside, begun 1888. Bournville, Birmingham, begun 1893. Letchworth, Herts, begun 1903; Wythenshawe, Manchester, begun 1927 (Sir Raymond Unwin). Welwyn Garden City, Herts, 1918-20 (Louis de Soissons & Arthur W. Kenyon). Hampstead Garden Suburb, London, 1908 (Sir Edwin Lutyens). Portmeirion, Gwynedd, 1926-59 (Clough Williams-Ellis). Harlow, Essex, begun 1947 (Frederick Gibberd). Croydon; Stevenage, Welwyn, Hatfield and Hemel Hempstead, Herts; Bracknell, Berks; Crawley, W. Sussex; Basildon, Essex; all resulting from British New Towns Act, 1946.

Postwar houses and housing

Frog Meadow, Dedham, Essex; villas at Regent's Park, London; Kingswaldenbury (Erith & Terry). Churchill Gardens, Pimlico, London (Powell & Moya). Alton West Estate, Roehampton, London (LCC Architects). Cluster Block Housing, Bethnal Green, London (Denys Lasdun). Barbican, City of London (Chamberlin Powell & Bon). Lillington Street, Pimlico, London (Darbourne & Darke). Park Hill, Sheffield (City Architects). Byker, Newcastle (Ralph Erskine). Robin Hood Gardens, London (A. & P. Smithson). Sutton Square and China Wharf, London (CZWG). Alexandra Road, London (Neave Brown). Friar's Quay, Norwich (Feilden & Mawson). St Mark's Road, London (Jeremy Dixon). Self-build houses at Lewisham, London (Walter Segal). Underhill, Peak District National Park (Arthur Quarmby). Lea View House, London (Hunt Thompson).

Postwar educational and cultural buildings

Queen Elizabeth Hall and Guildhall, London (Sir Giles Gilbert Scott). York University (Sir Robert Matthew). Coventry Cathedral; Sussex University (Sir Basil Spence). Royal College of Physicians and National Theatre, London; University of East Anglia, Norwich (Sir Denys Lasdun). Faculty of Engineering, Leicester; Sealey Library, Cambridge; Florey Building, Oxford; Clore Extension to Tate Gallery (Sir James Stirling). Sainsbury Centre for the Arts, Norwich; Sackler Gallery, Royal Academy (Sir Norman Foster). Mound Stand, Lord's Cricket Ground, London; Glyndebourne Opera House, East Sussex (Michael Hopkins & Partners). Minster Lovell Mill Study Centre, Oxon; Fountains Visitor Centre, Fountains Abbey, N. Yorks; University of East London Campus; Centre for Mathematical Sciences, Cambridge University (Edward Cullinan). Cripps Building, St John's College, Cambridge; Festival Theatre, Chichester; Museum of London (Powell & Moya). Bowra Building and St John's College, Oxford; Blue Boar Court, Cambridge; the Ruskin Library, Lancaster (MacCormac Jamieson & Pritchard). Hatch Warren Junior and Woodlea Primary Schools (Hampshire County Architects). Hunstanton School, Norfolk (A. & P. Smithson). Royal Festival Hall, London (GLC Architects). St Catherine's College, Oxford (Arne Jacobsen). Aviary at London Zoo (Cedric Price, Lord Snowdon and Frank Newby). Department of Electrical Engineering, Liverpool (Yorke Rosenberg Mardall). Liverpool Catholic Cathedral; Central London Mosque, Regent's Park, London (Frederick Gibberd). Royal Exchange Theatre, Manchester (Levitt Bernstein). British Library, London (Colin St John Wilson). CDT Building, Bryanston, Dorset (CZWG). Cirencester College of Agriculture, Glos (David Lea). Princess of Wales Conservatory, Kew, Surrey (PSA). Leeds Castle Grotto, Kent (Vernon Gibberd). Courts of Justice, Truro, Cornwall (Evans & Shalev). Brentwood Cathedral (Quinlan Terry). Contact Theatre, Manchester (Short & Associates). The Millennium Centre, Dagenham (Penoyre & Prasad).

The Millennium Dome, London (Richard Rogers Partnership). The Millennium Bridge, London; The Great Glass House, Llanarthney, Carmarthenshire, Wales (Foster & Partners). The Tate Modern, London (Herzog & de Meuron). The London Eye, London (Marks Barfield). International Centre for Life, Newcastle (Terry Farrell & Partners). Peckham Library, London (Will Alsop). Media Centre for Marylebone Cricket Club (Future Systems). Lowry Centre, Salford (Michael Wilford). Royal Victoria Dock Bridge, London (Lifschutz Davidson). The Landmark, Ilfracombe (Tim Ronalds). Museum of Scotland, Edinburgh (Benson & Forsyth). Rare Books Repository, Newnham College, Cambridge (van Heyningen & Haward). Post-graduate Study Centre, Darwin College, Cambridge (Dixon Jones).

Postwar industrial, commercial and office buildings (1945 onwards)

Inmos Microprocessor Factory, Newport; Renault Centre, Swindon; Lloyd's Building, London (Sir Richard Rogers). Willis Faber Dumas, Ipswich; Stockley Park, Heathrow, London; Stansted Airport Terminal, Essex (Sir Norman Foster). TV am; Alban Gate; Embankment Place (all London; Terry Farrell). Schlumberger Research Centre, Cambridge; David Mellor Cutlery Factory, Hathersage, Derbyshire; Bracken House, London; Portcullis House and Westminster Station, London; Inland Revenue HQ, Nottingham (Michael Hopkins & Partners). Financial Times Printing Works, London; Western Morning News HQ, Plymouth; Waterloo International Terminal, London (Nicholas Grimshaw). Dufours Place, Soho, London; Richmond Riverside, Surrey (Quinlan Terry). Chilworth Science Park, Southampton; RMC HQ, Egham, Surrey (Edward Cullinan). Dunlop Factory, Brynmawr, Gwent (Architects Co-Partnership). Economist Building, London (A. & P. Smithson). Post Office Tower, London (Sir Eric Bedford). New Zealand House, London (Sir Robert Matthew). Wood Street Police Station, London (McMorran & Whitby). Reliance Controls Factory, Swindon (Team 4). Commercial Union Tower, London (Gollins, Melvin Ward). Hillingdon Civic Centre, Middlesex (Andrew Derbyshire). Thames Barrier, London (GLC Architects). Broadgate, London (Arup Associates). Pumping Station, Isle of Dogs (John Outram). Richmond House, Whitehall (William Whitfield). Epping DC Offices, Essex (Richard Reid). Victoria Quarter, Leeds (Derek Latham). The Ark, Hammersmith, London (Ralph Erskine). Canary Wharf Tower, London (Cesar Pelli). St Mary's Hospital, Isle of Wight (Ahrends, Burton & Koralek). Electronic Arts HQ, Surrey (Foster & Partners).

Further reading

Adam, Robert. *Classical Architecture*. Viking, 1992.

Archer, Lucy. *Architecture in Britain and Ireland 600–1500*. The Harvill Press, 1999.

Breckon, B., and Parker, J. *Tracing the History of Houses*. Countryside Books, 2000.

Brunskill, R.W. *Vernacular Architecture: An Illustrated Handbook*. Faber & Faber, 2000.

Ching, Francis D.K. *A Visual Dictionary of Architecture*. John Wiley & Sons, 1997.

Clifton-Taylor, Alec. *The Pattern of English Building*. Faber & Faber, 1987.

Colvin, Howard. *A Biographical Dictionary of British Architects 1600–1840*. Yale, 1995.

Cooper, Nicholas. *Houses of the Gentry 1480–1680*. Yale/English Heritage, 1999.

Cornforth, John. *The Country Houses of England 1948–1998*. Constable, 1998.

Curl, James Stevens. *Encyclopedia of Architectural Terms*. Donhead, 1992.

Davey, Peter. *Arts and Crafts Architecture*. Phaidon, 1999.

Fleming, J., Honour, H., and Pevsner, N. *Penguin Dictionary of Architecture and Landscape Architecture*. Penguin Books, 1998.

Frampton, Kenneth. *Modern Architecture: A Critical History*. Thames & Hudson, 1997.

Glancey, Jonathan. *Twentieth Century Architecture – The Structures That Shaped the Century*. Carlton Books, 1998.

Gore, Alan and Ann. *The History of English Interiors*. Phaidon, 1991.

Green, Candida Lycett. *Country Life 100 Favourite Houses*. Boxtree, 1999.

Hall, Michael. *The English Country House 1897–1939*. Mitchell Beazley, 1994.

Hitchcock, Henry-Russell. *Modern Architecture: Romanticism and Reintegration*. Da Capo Press, 1993.

Jencks, Charles. *The Language of Post-Modern Architecture*. Academy Editions, 1991.

Jenkins, Simon. *England's 1000 Best Churches*. Allen Lane/The Penguin Press, 1999.

Kaufmann, Emil. *Architecture in the Age of Reason*. Dover Publications, 1968.

Le Corbusier. *Towards a New Architecture*. Architectural Press, 1999.

Lloyd, Nathaniel. *A History of English Brickwork*. Antique Collectors' Club, reprinting 2001.

Montgomery-Massingberd, Hugh. *Great Houses of Scotland*. Laurence King, 1997.

Newton, Miranda. *Architects' London Houses*. Butterworth Architecture, 1992.

Norberg-Schultz, Christian. *Principles of Modern Architecture*. Andreas Papadakis Publishing, 2000.

Pearman, Hugh. *Contemporary World Architecture*. Phaidon, 1998.

Pevsner Architectural Guides: The Buildings of England. (A county by county series of volumes, also extending to Scotland.) Penguin Books, 1951 to date.

Pragnell, Hubert. *Britain: A Guide to Architectural Styles from 1066 to the Present Day*. Ellipsis London Ltd, 1999.

Quiney, Anthony. *The Traditional Buildings of England*. Thames & Hudson, 1990.

St John Wilson, Colin. *Architectural Reflections*. Butterworth Architecture, 1992.

Sharp, Dennis. *A Visual History of Twentieth Century Architecture*. Lund Humphries, 1991.

Watkin, David. *A History of Western Architecture*. Laurence King Publishing, 1996.

Watkin, David. *English Architecture*. Thames & Hudson, 1997.

Weinreb, Matthew. *London Architecture Features and Facades*. Phaidon, 1993.

Wittkower, Rudolf. *Architectural Principles in the Age of Humanism*. Academy Editions, 1998.

Worsley, Giles. *Classical Architecture in Britain – The Heroic Age*. Paul Mellon Centre for Studies in British Art, 1995.

Index

150